THE ART OF THE BRICK®

THE PICTORIAL

Nathan Sawaya

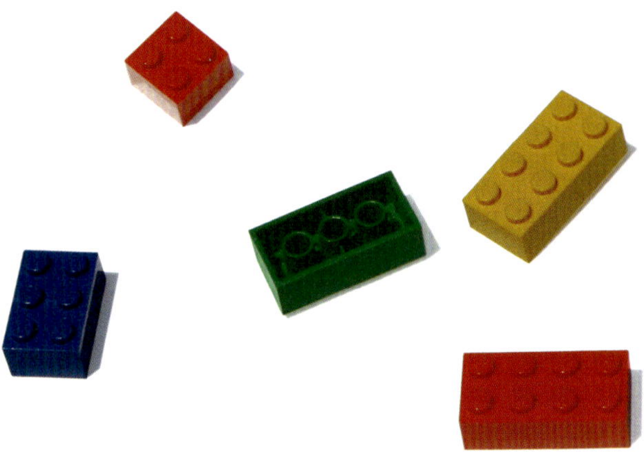

Second edition.

Design & Layout: Evelyn G. Epstein Associates, Inc. Lancaster, PA

Inset photo of Gray by Stephanie Mitchell. Photo of Tall Pencil by Larry Burton.

ISBN:

978-0-557-63226-8

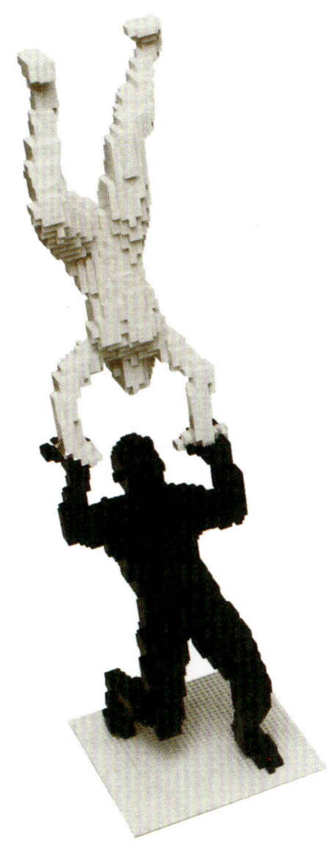

This book has photos of some of my sculptures.
Some are commercial, some are expressive and some are whimsical.
Just like me.

Enjoy.

Nathan Sawaya

For more information on Nathan's work, please go to www.brickartist.com or email him at nathan@brickartist.com.

Special thanks to Courtney for her dedication and commitment
to *The Art of the Brick*, this book and me.

Thanks also to:

Don Blyler, III for setting the tone

Scott Jones for the words and the burgers

Cindi Morrison for her vision

My sister for being younger

My dad for years of stepping on bricks

My mom for countless vacuum cleaners

To everyone who commissions my art

And a big shout out to a company in Denmark with supportive folks on both sides of the pond.

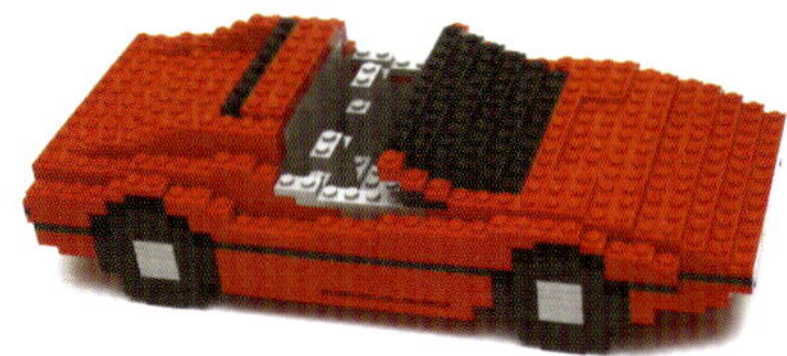

Table Of Contents:

THE ART OF THE BRICK: how to approach Nathan Sawaya's artwork

It's hard not to look at Nathan Sawaya's sculptures and privately think, "Hey, I could do that."

Or, "My six-year-old is also a really awesome LEGO® builder. Maybe he can have a museum show some day."

Or, "You know, I myself built some pretty terrific things out of LEGO in my day."

Or, "What's all the hoo-hah about? So what if some weird crackpot built some things out of LEGO? Who cares?"

Don't be embarrassed. It's natural to think these things. It's perfectly OK.

LEGO is usually found in toy stores. And the only contact most parents/adults have with LEGO is when they step on a stray brick in the middle of the night. But if you're looking at Sawaya's pieces while thinking one or all of the above thoughts, then you're not seeing things clearly. You're going to have to put your nostalgia aside. And put your LEGO bias aside. You're going to have to open your mind a little and try to see beyond the LEGO bricks.

After all, you don't look at Roy Lichenstein's work and think, "Nice comics." You don't look at something by Warhol and say, "That reminds me, I need to pick up some a few cans of minestrone on the way home." Look at the architecture in Sawaya's pieces. Look at the craft involved. Look at the intricate brick work. Look at how Sawaya has managed to create organic-looking sculptures that defy and celebrate the very medium they're created in at the same time.

Sawaya is a surrealist mash-up of forms and artists. Imagine Frank Lloyd Wright crossed with Ray Harryhausen, or Auguste Rodin crossed with Shigeru Miyamoto, and you start to get a sense of where Sawaya is coming from.

Because of the nature of the medium, you're likely going to want to touch Sawaya's sculptures. (I strongly advise not doing so, unless you'd like your day at the museum to be cut short.) Why? Call it the gravitas of LEGO.

It's nearly impossible to look at something created out of LEGO and not want to start building yourself. It's almost as if your fingers remember what it's like to hold those plastic bricks in your hand. Close your eyes for a second, and you can practically hear the sound of two bricks fitting together with that almost primordial LEGO snap. There's something immensely comforting in that snap. It's the sound of everything fitting together perfectly. Taking things a step further, it's the sound of the world making sense for one, brief moment.

Beyond setting aside your own memories and LEGO bias, get yourself a bucket of LEGO bricks. Sink your hands into the bucket. Snap a few bricks together. (Trust me, it's better than any anti-depressant.)

Only then will you truly appreciate the magnificent works you are about to see.

Scott Jones

Scott Jones is a writer based in New York City.

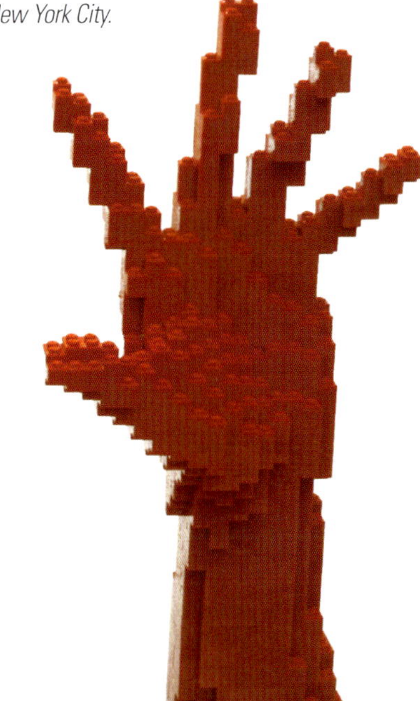

Brick Art Collection

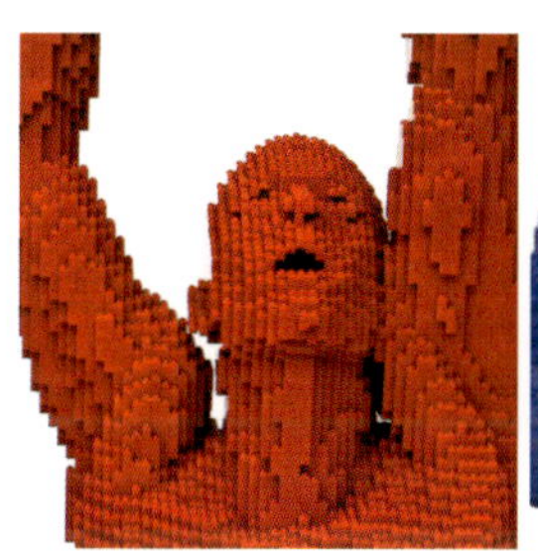
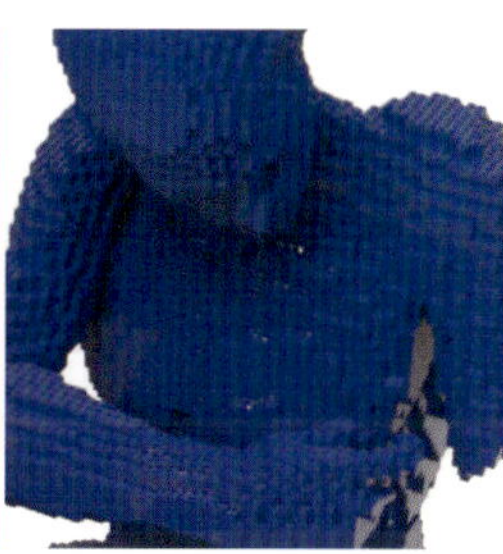
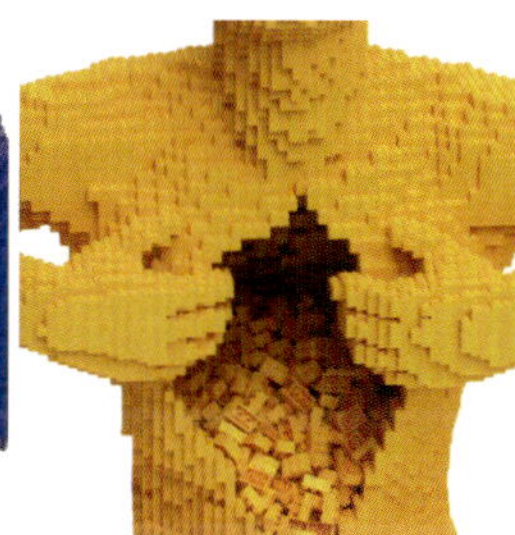
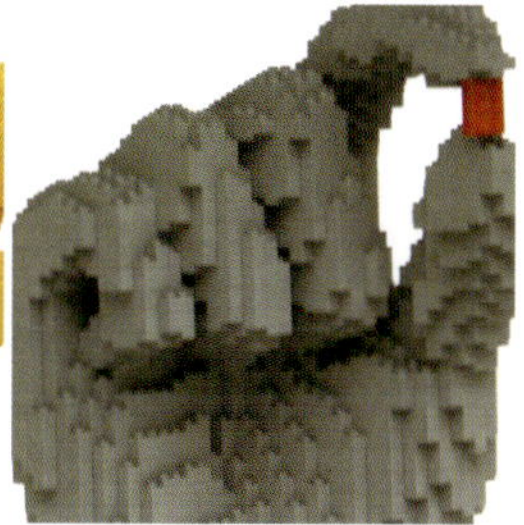

Mask
29" x 71" x 24"

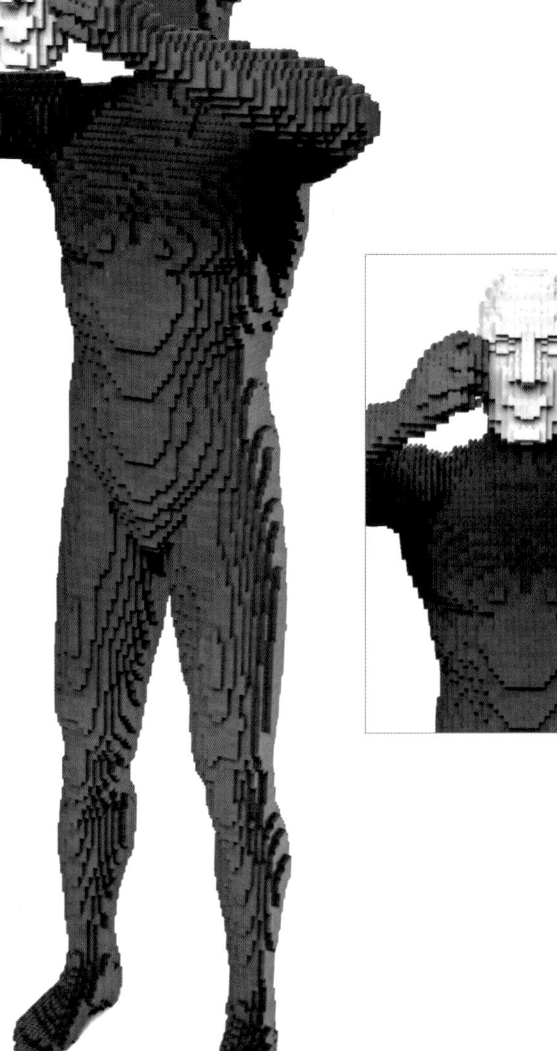

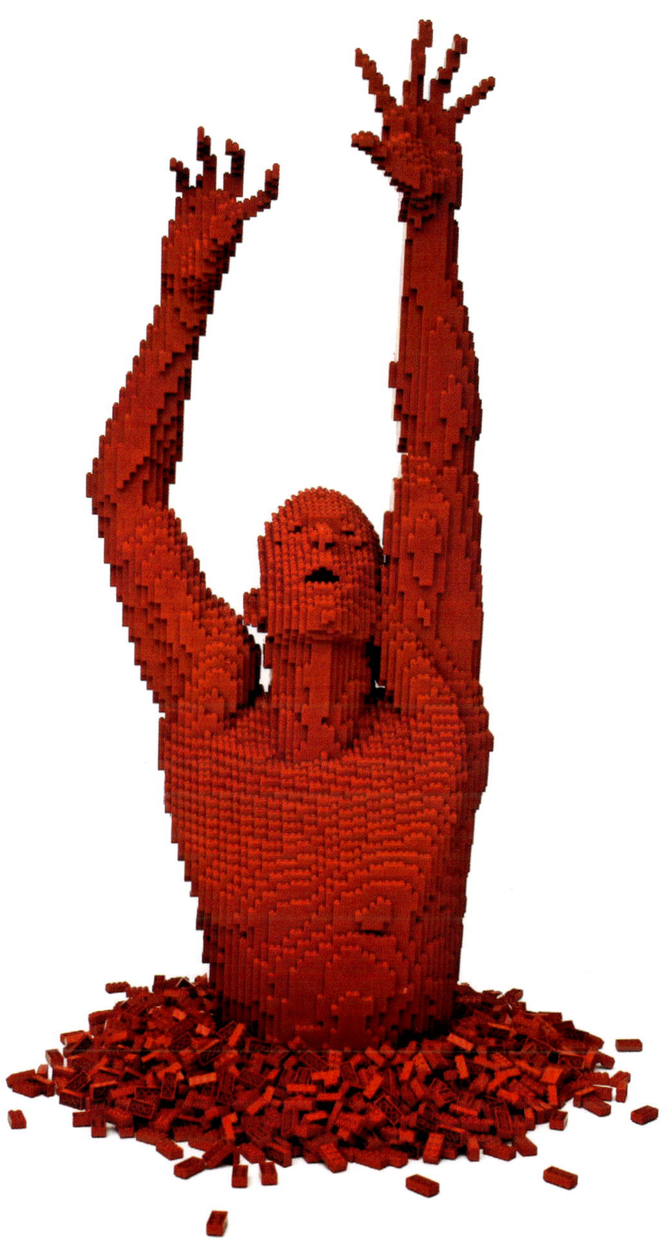

Red
24″ x 49″ x 26″

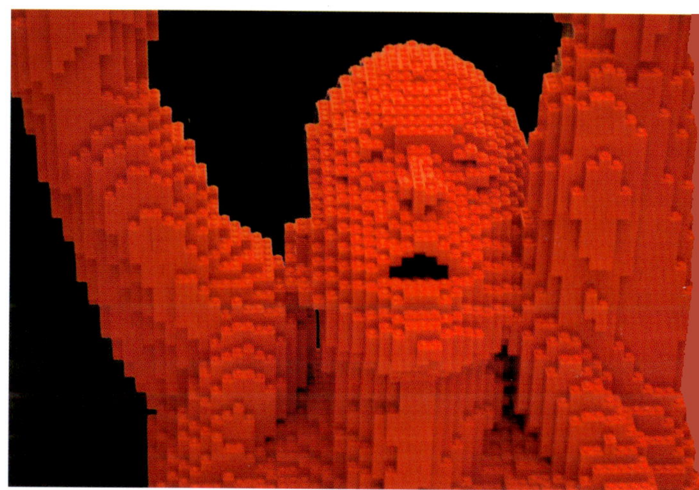

Red represents a transition in life. I leave it up to you as to whether the figure is sinking or rising. Or just lounging in bricks.

Yellow
35″ x 13″ x 28″

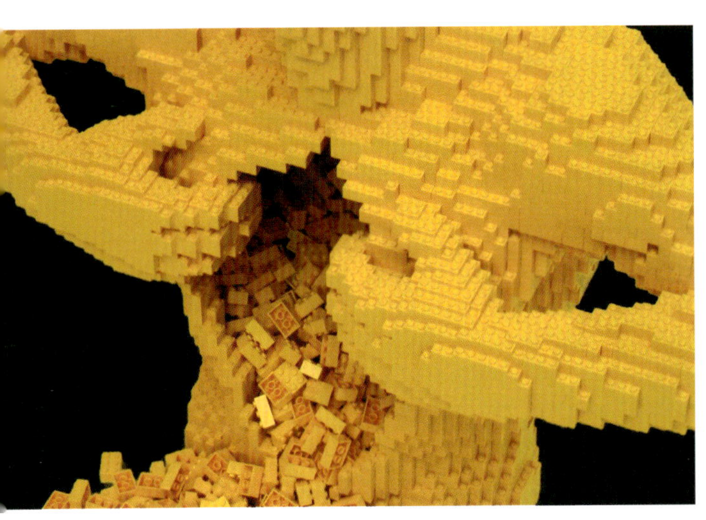

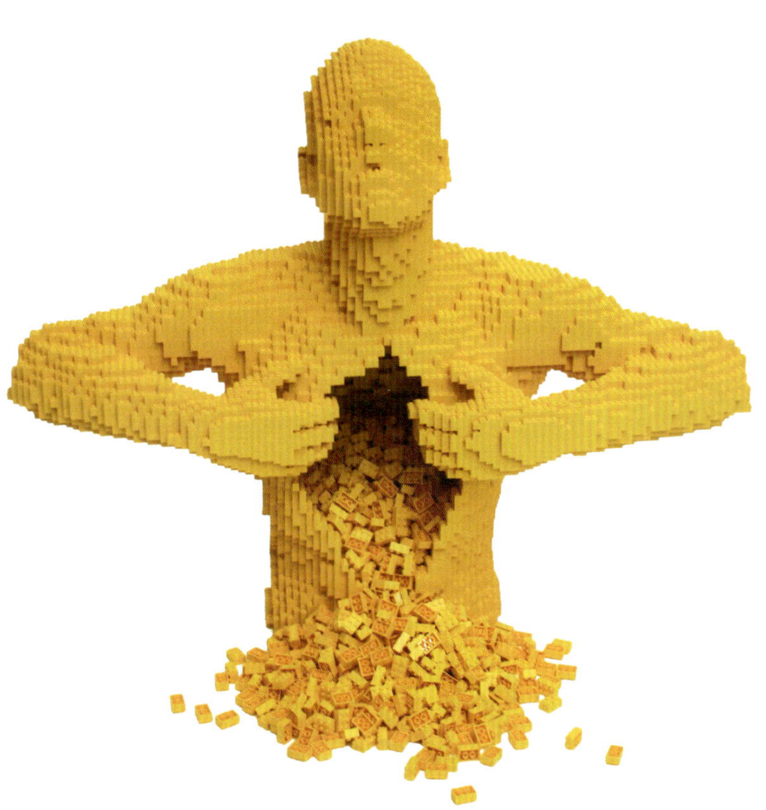

Opening oneself up to the world is not an easy thing to do.

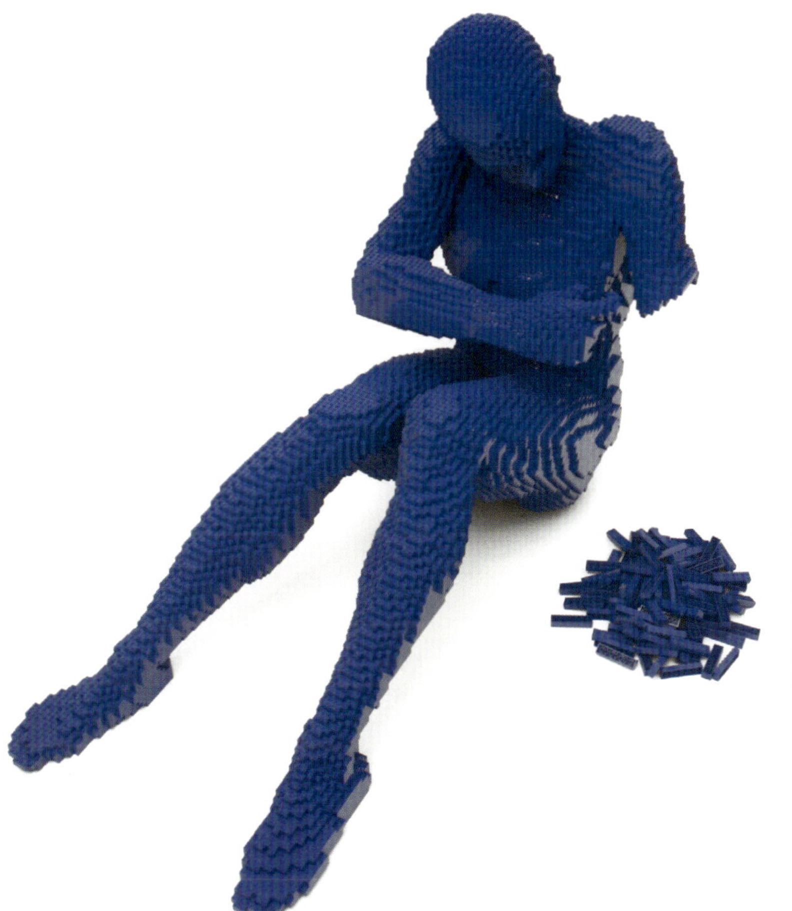

Blue
42″ x 34″ x 18″

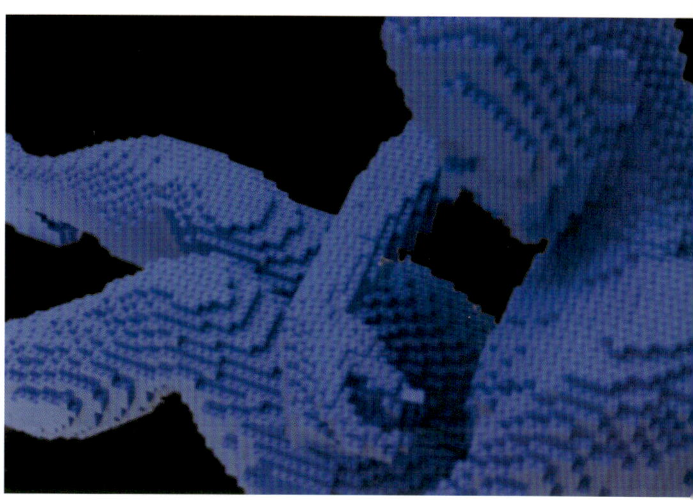

A self-made man? Or taking himself apart? I'll never tell. Unless someone was to start taking my arm apart piece by piece.

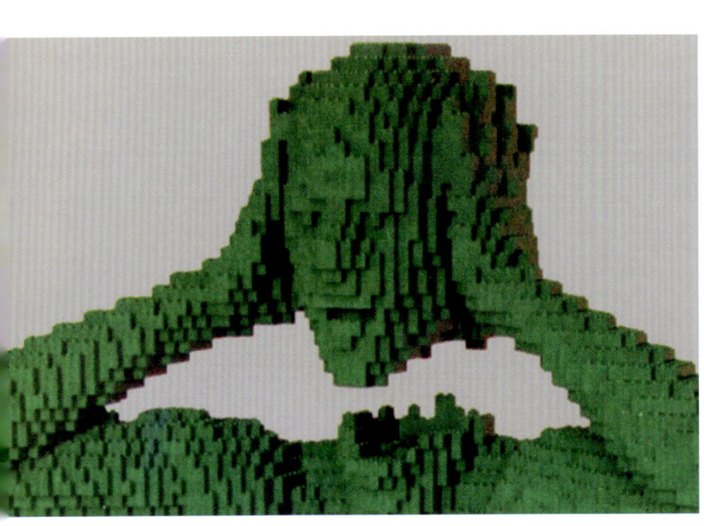

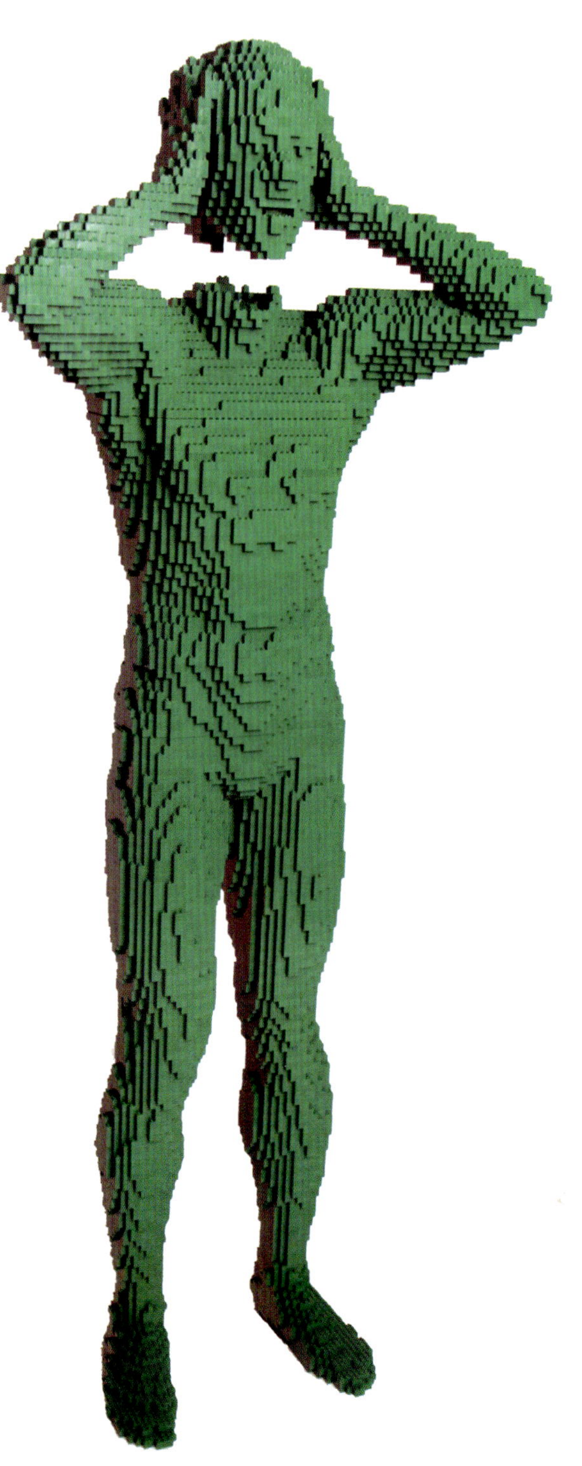

Green
27" x 70" x 15"

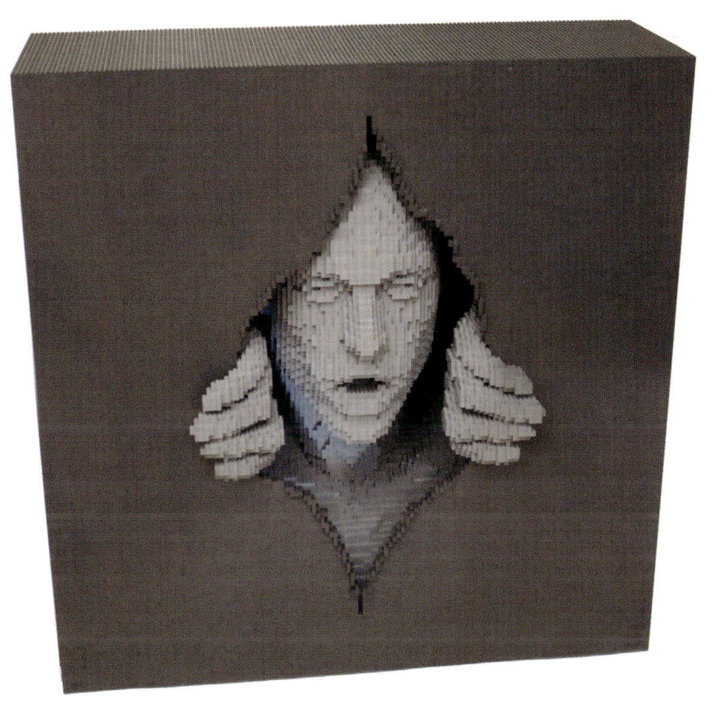

Gray
45″ x 45″ x 15″

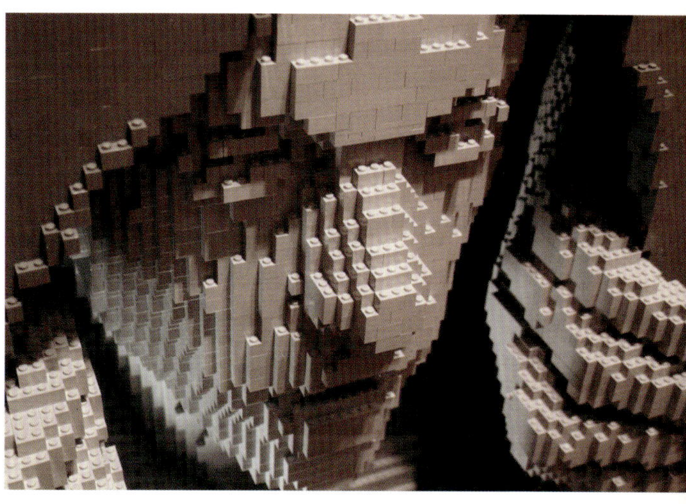

A lot of folks ask me if Gray was inspired from a metamorphosis representing an emergence from depression, but I think it was inspired from the time I was trapped in a box.

Overcome
27" x 42" x 24"

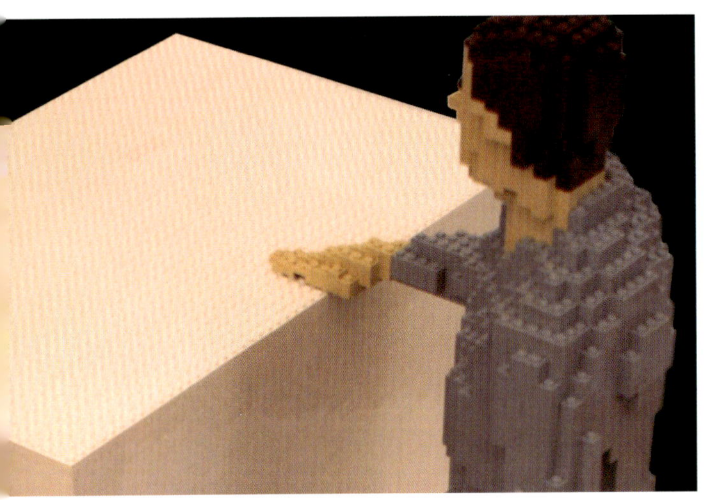

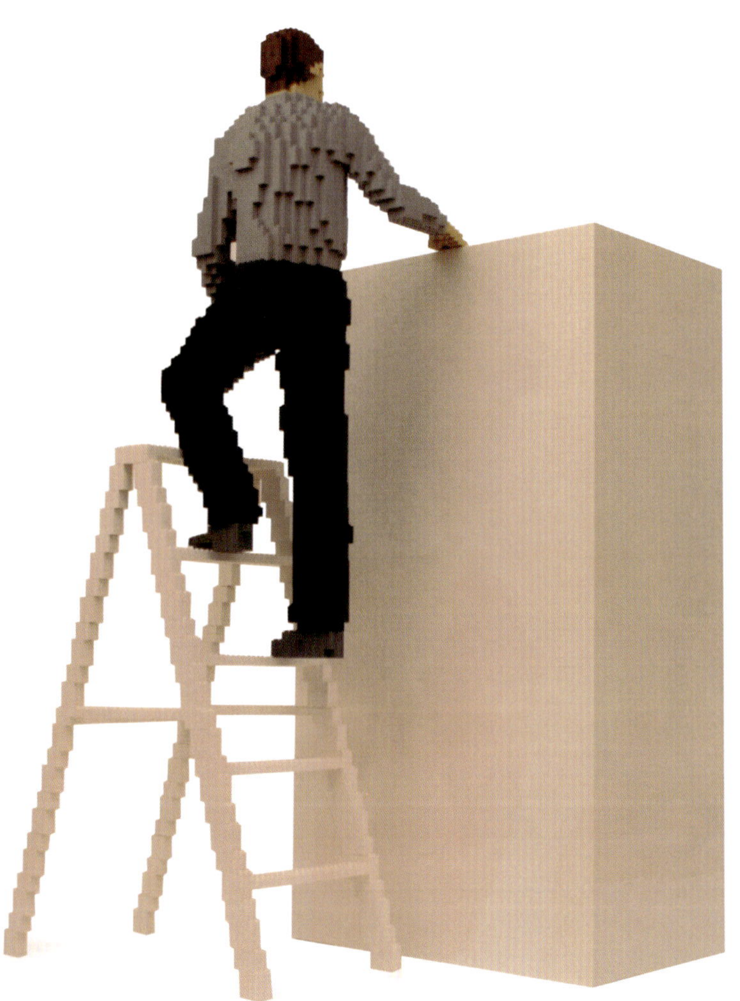

Overcoming obstacles is an important part of brick art.

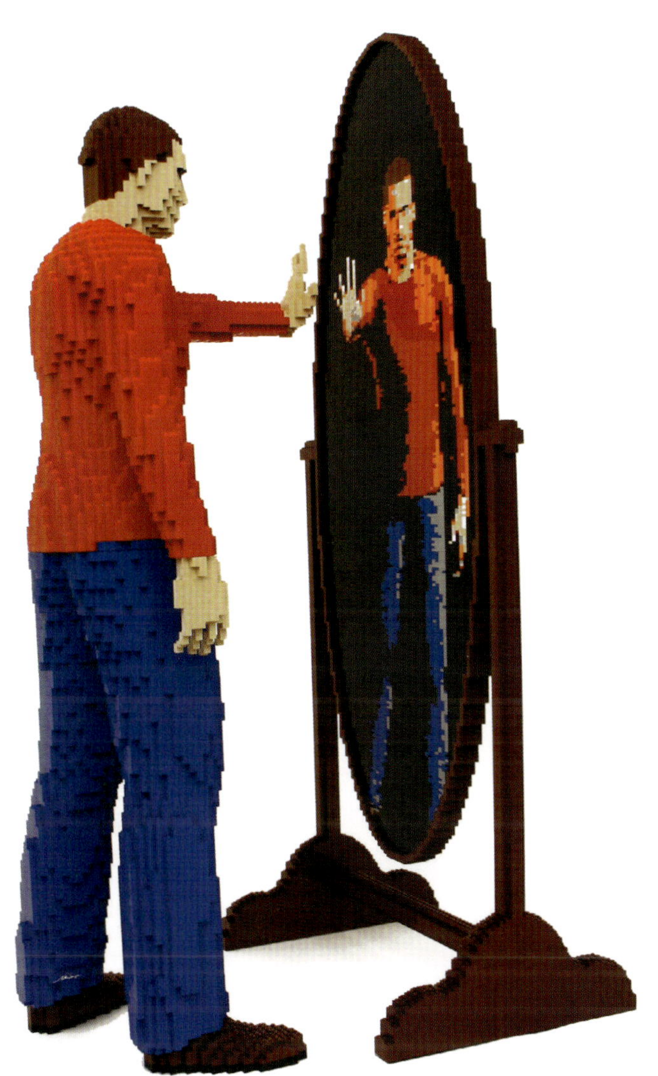

Reflection
28″ x 48″ x 20″

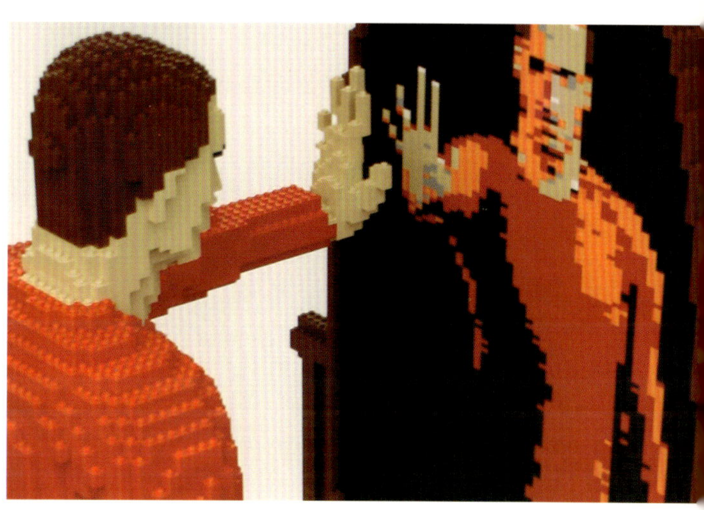

Seeing oneself in brick.

Tall Pencil
14″ x 93″ x 14″

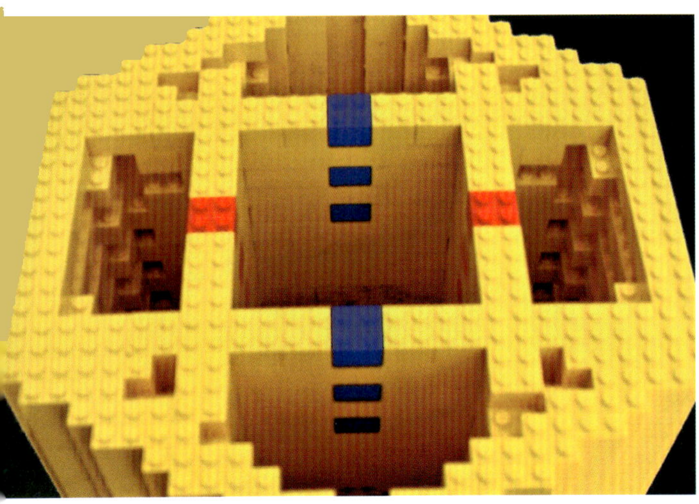

I used over 20,000 bricks on the Tall Pencil.

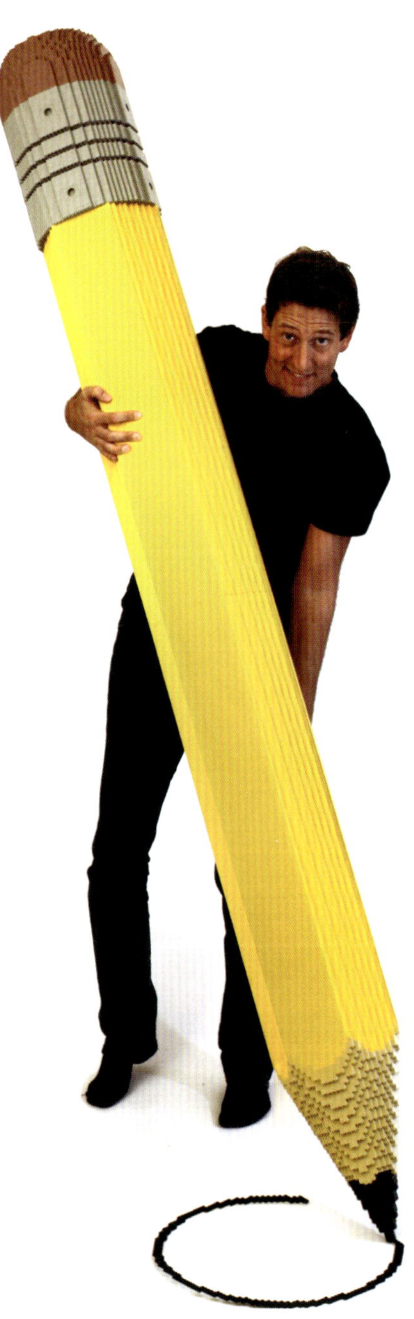

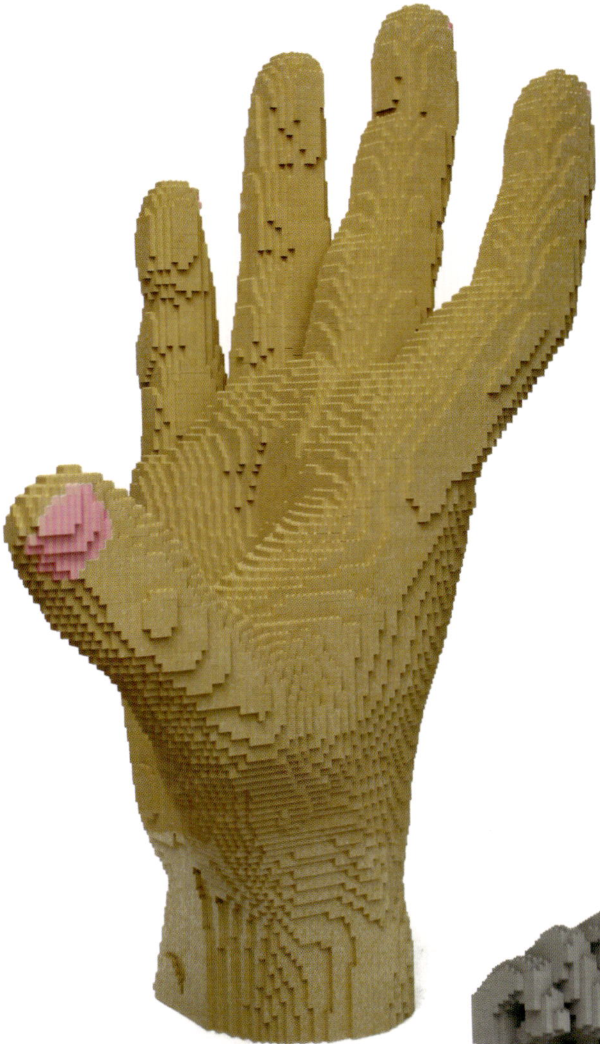

Hand
31″ x 54″ x 37″

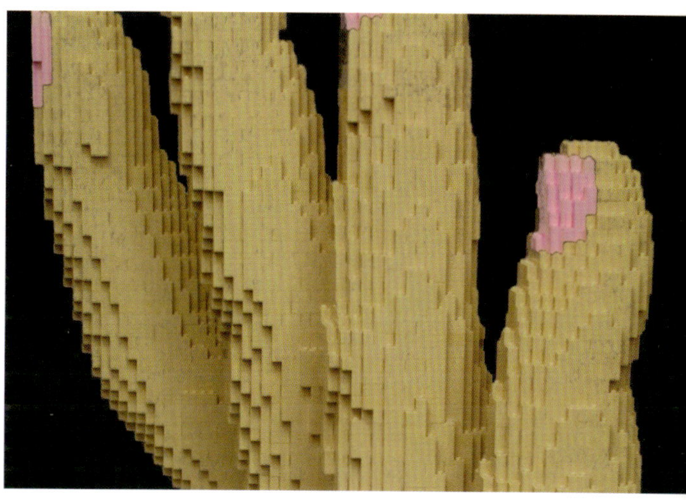

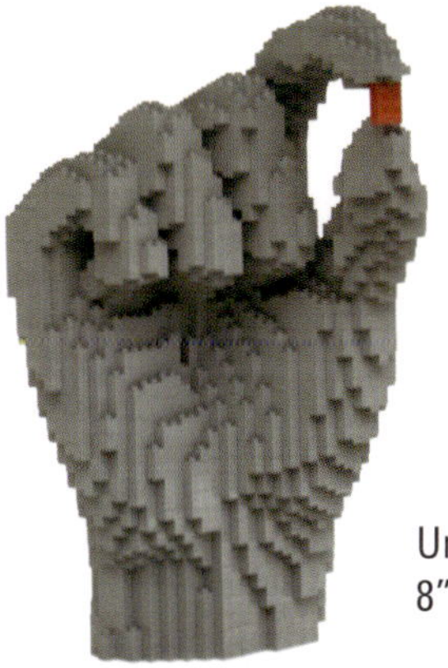

Untitled
8″ x 15″ x 7″

An Artist's View
75" x 58" x 75"

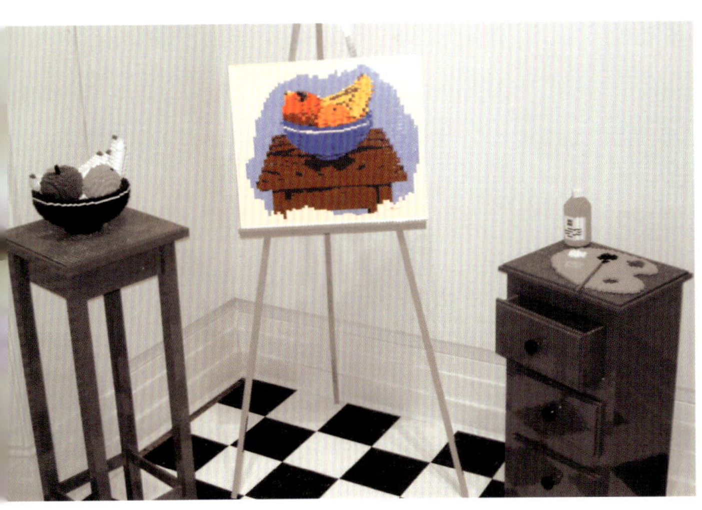

No, it's not a black and white photo.

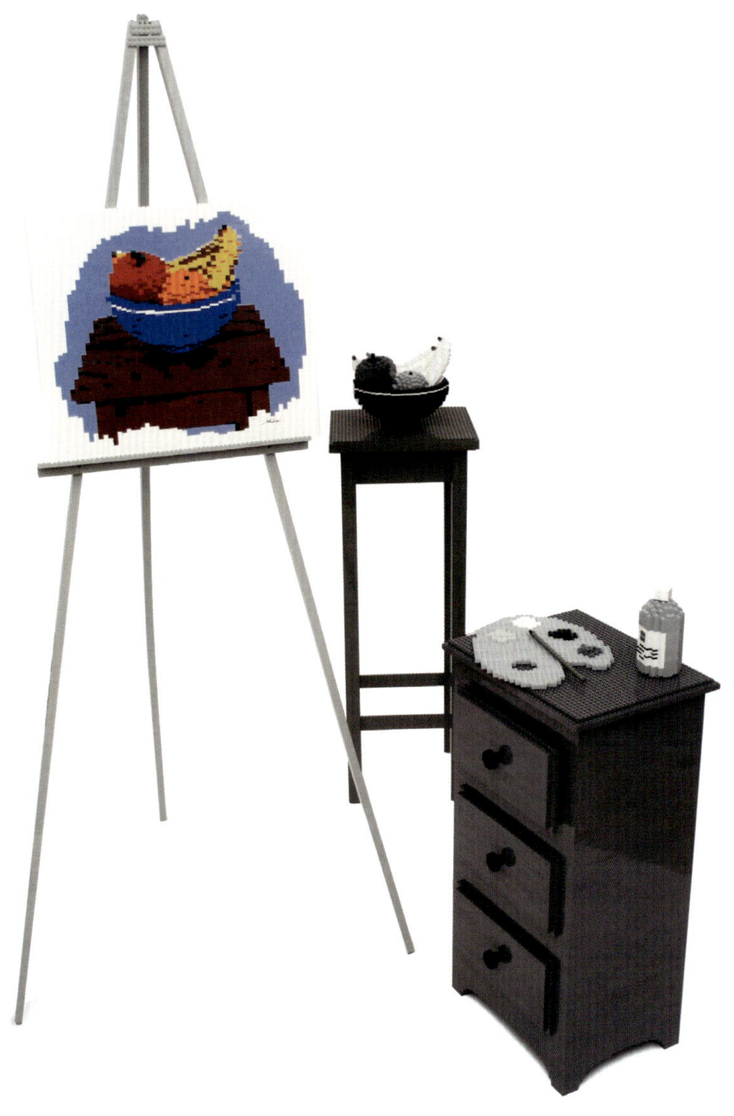

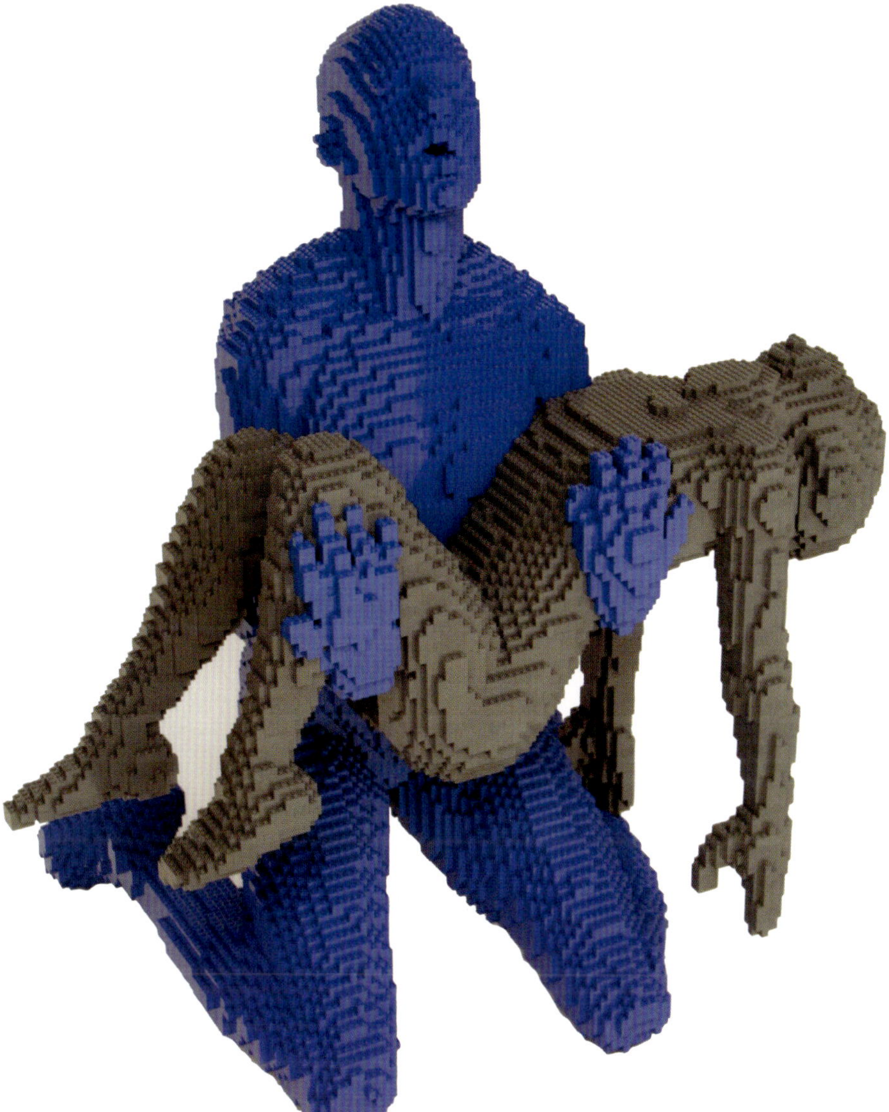

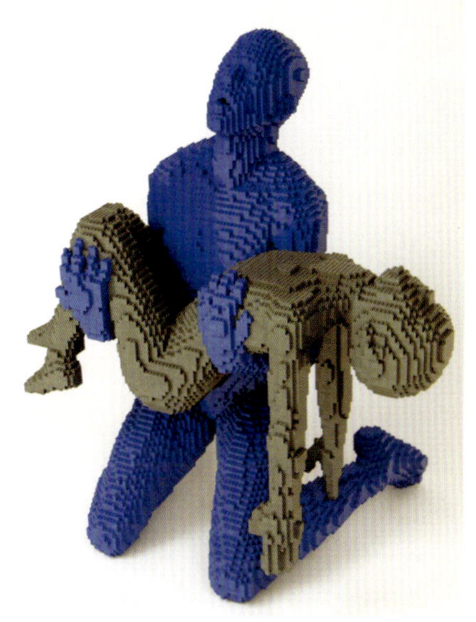

My Boy
41" x 28" x 24"

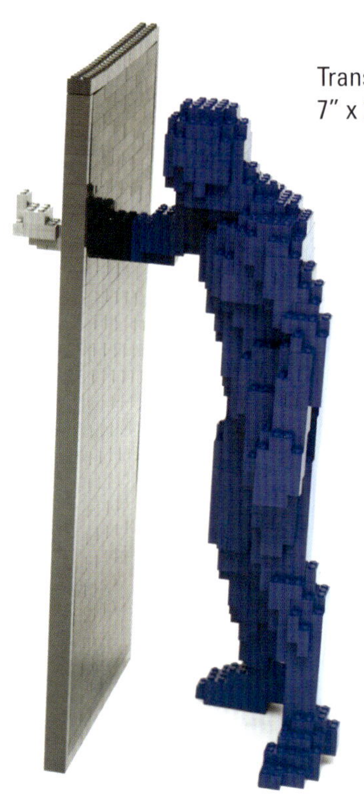

Transition
7″ x 21″ x 6″

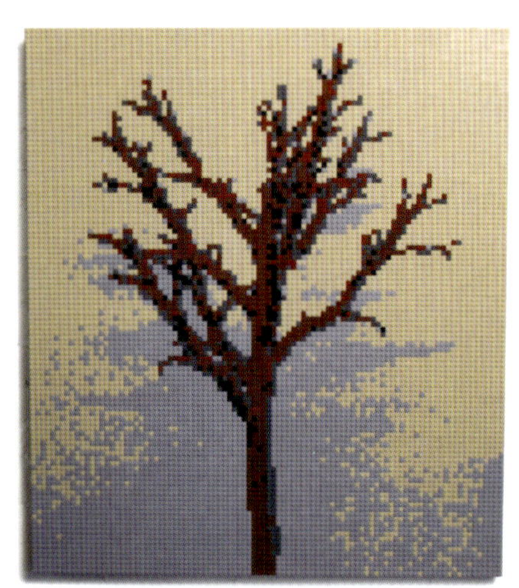

Tree Shadow
30″ x 38″

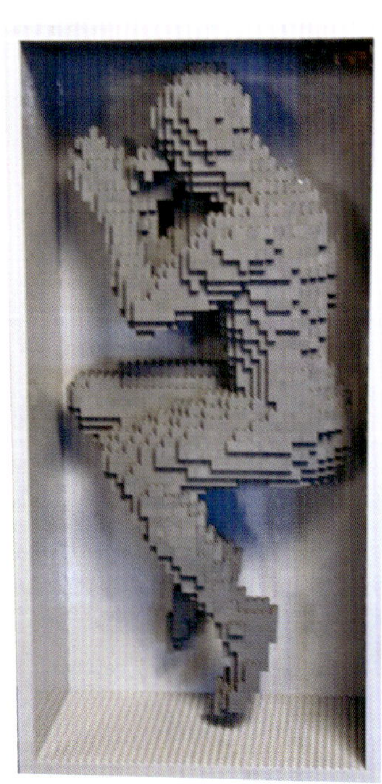

Womb
22″ x 31″ x 19″

Tree
18″x 38″ x 18″

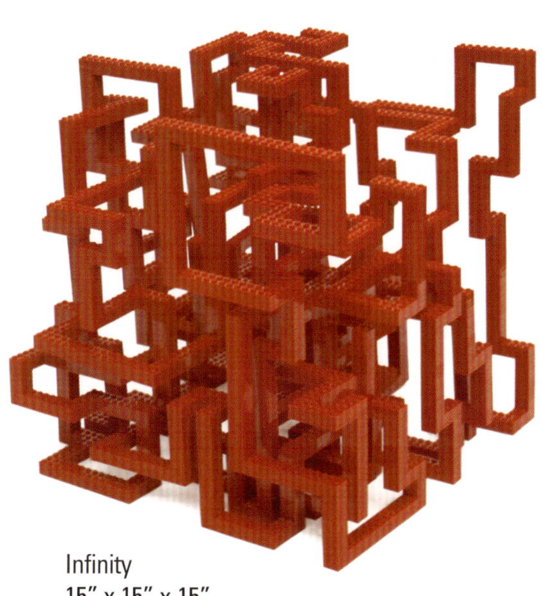

Infinity
15″ x 15″ x 15″

The sculpture is one continuous red line that at no point touches itself.

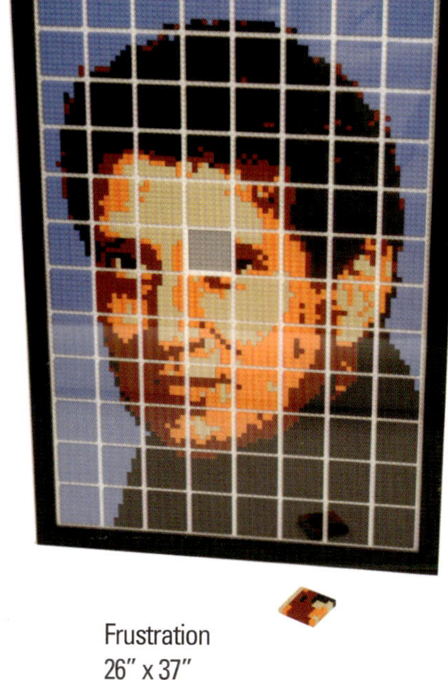

Frustration
26″ x 37″

Sing
31″ x 56″ x 15″

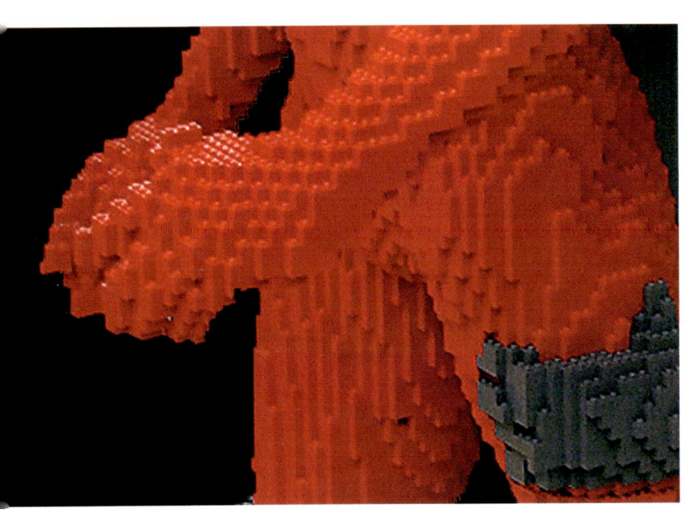

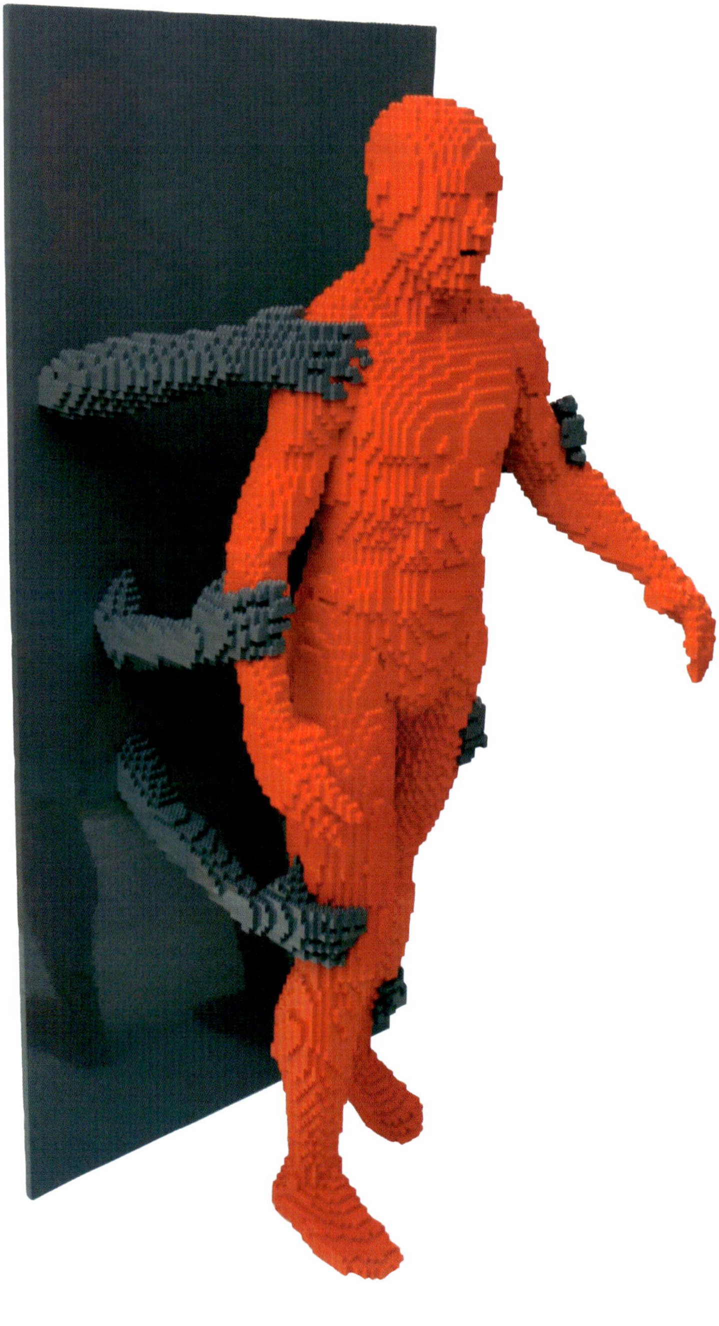

Grasp
30″ x 67″ x 30″

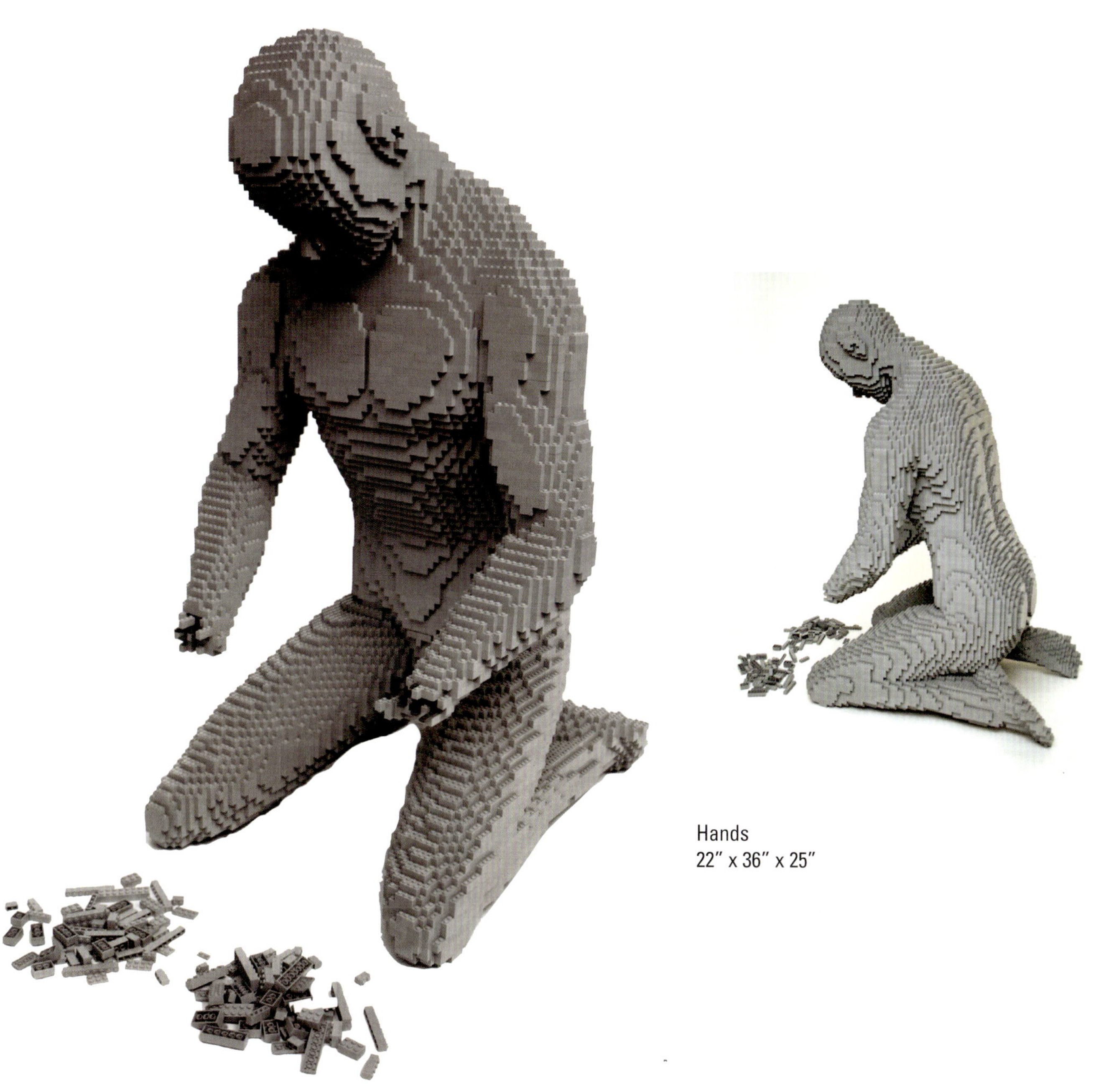

Hands
22″ x 36″ x 25″

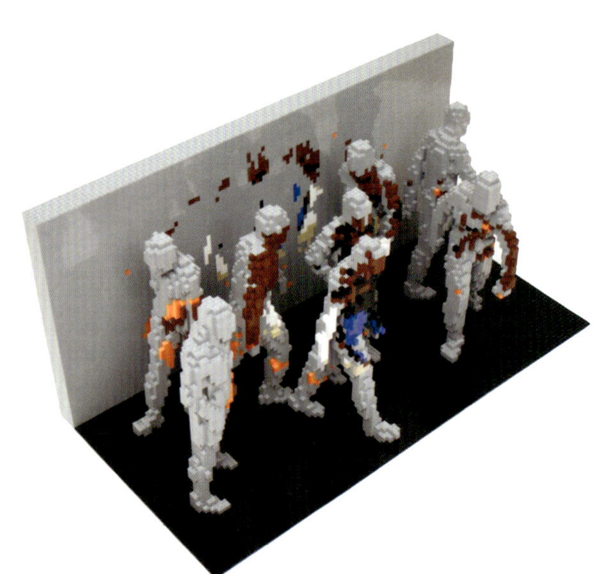

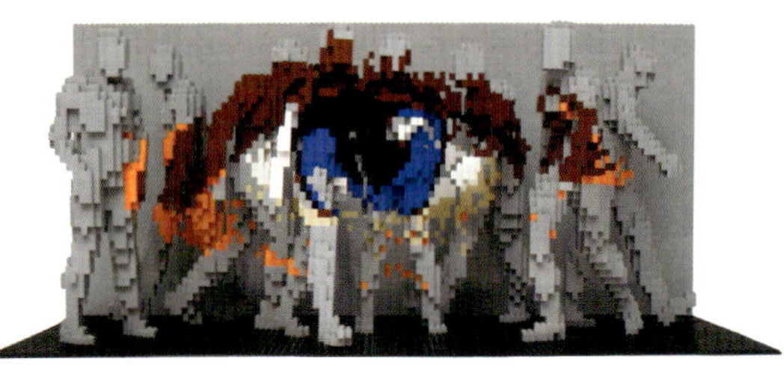

Crowd
18″ x 17″ x 37″

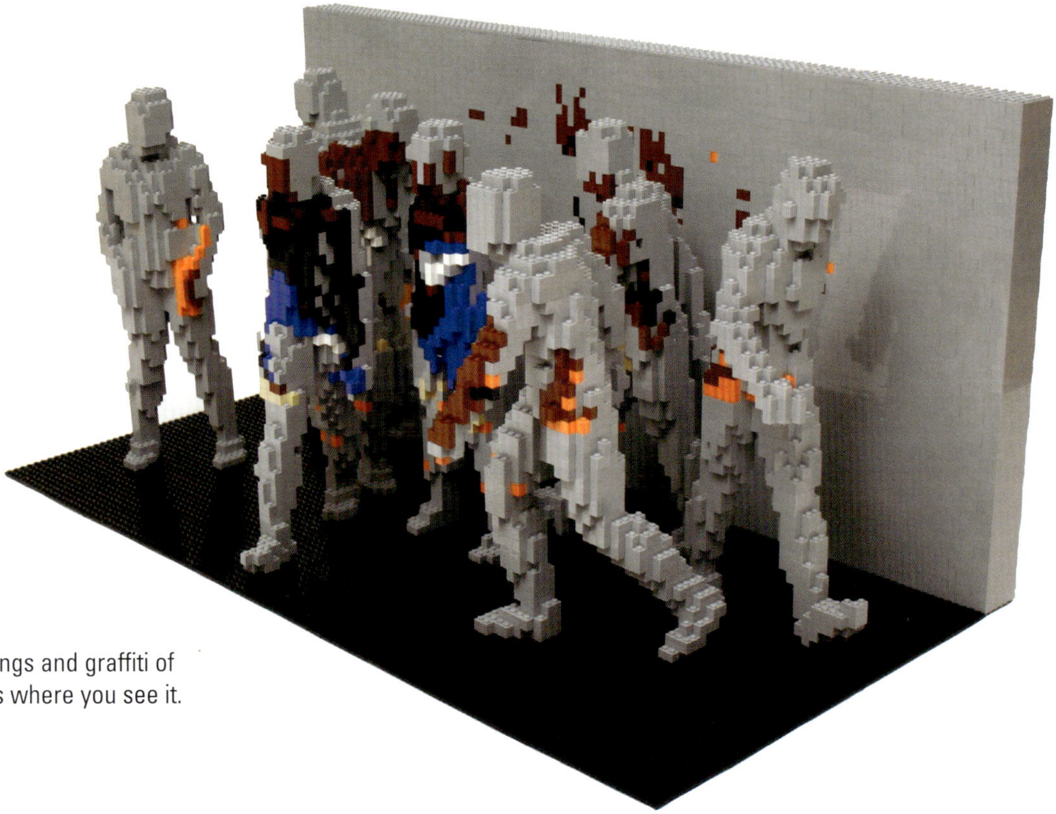

Inspired by the throngs and graffiti of New York City; art is where you see it.

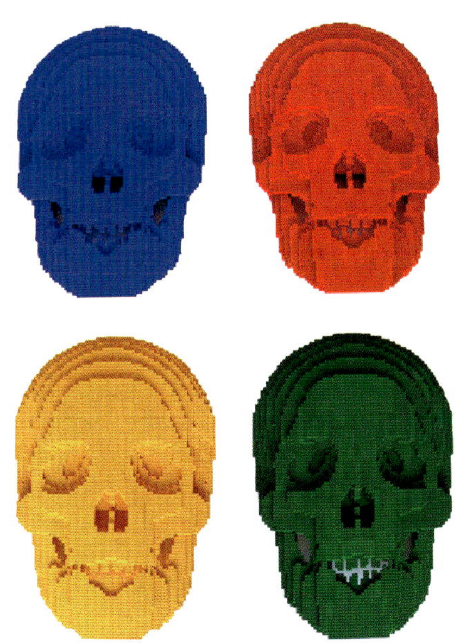

Skulls
54″ x 74″ x 4″

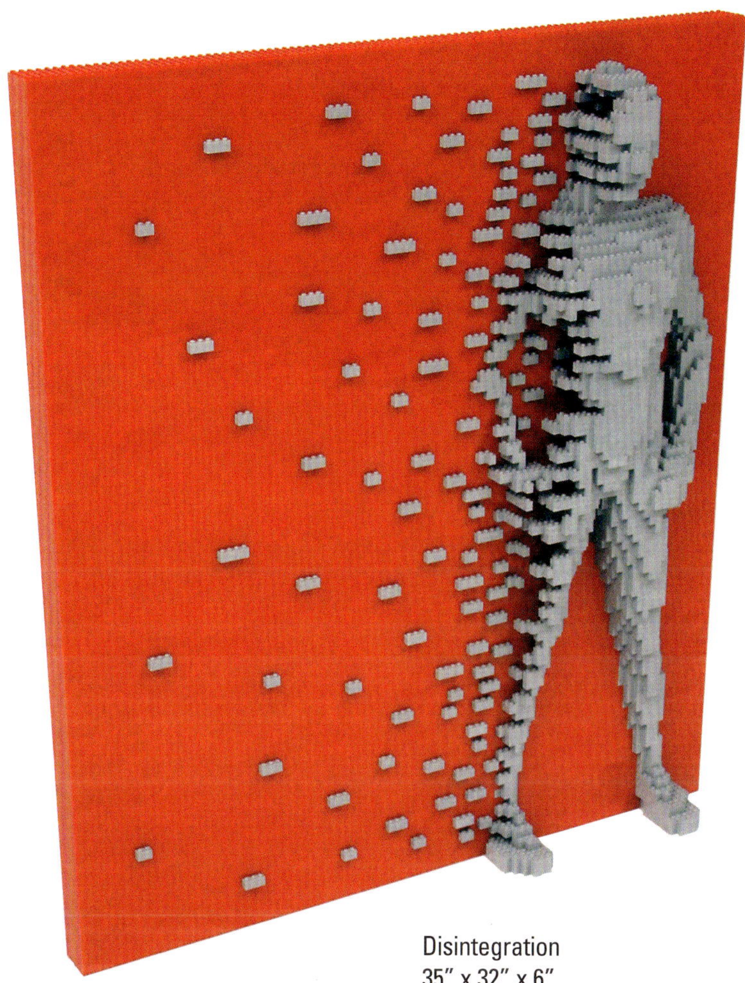

Disintegration
35″ x 32″ x 6″

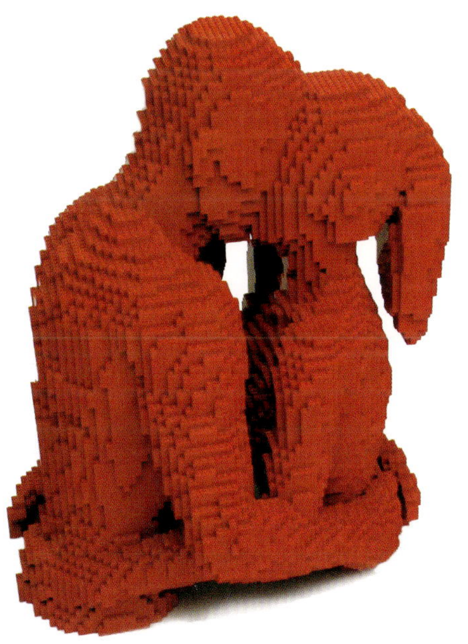

Kiss
27″ x 21″ x 20″

Peace by Pieces
30″ x 30″ x 4″

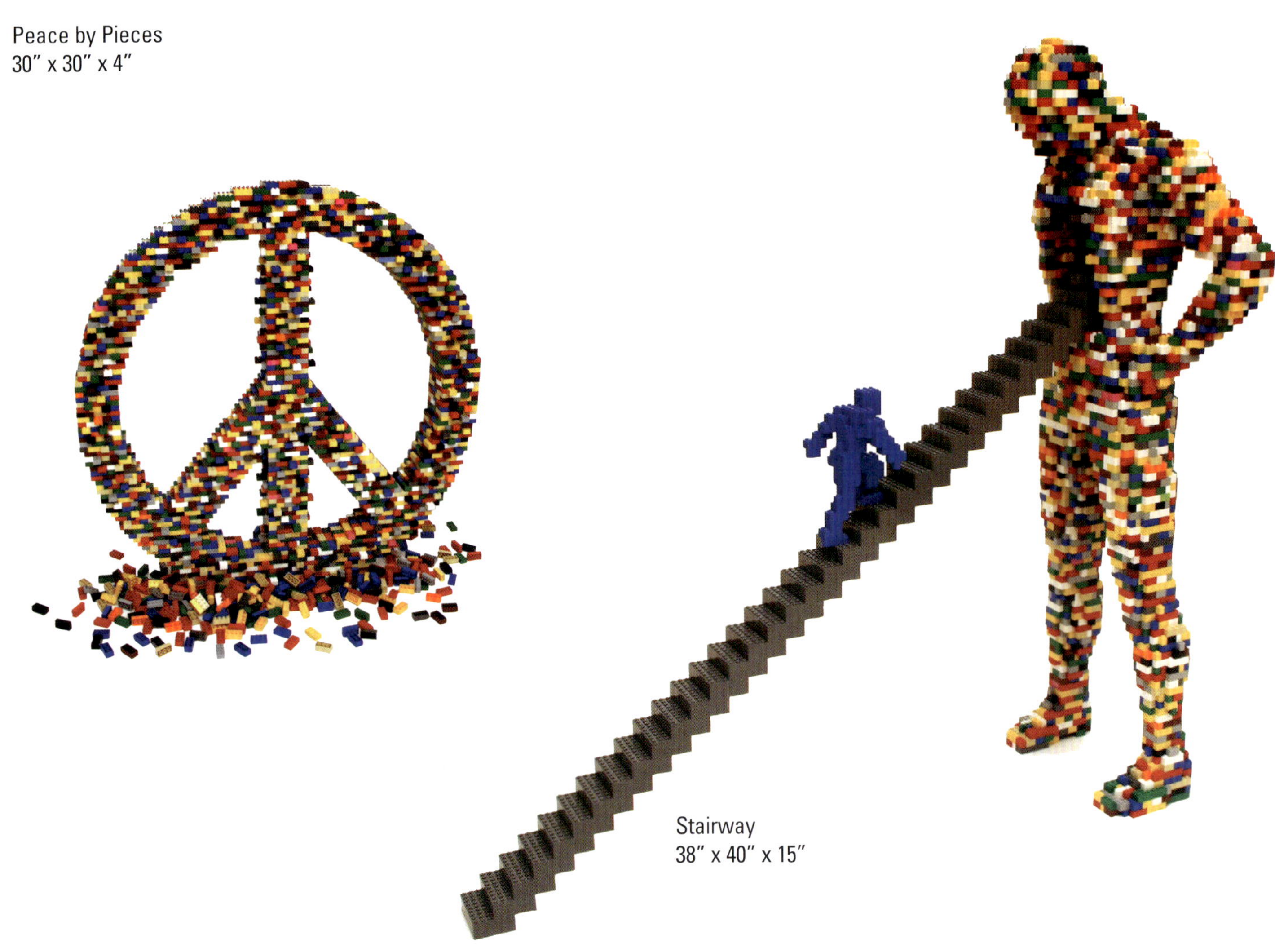

Stairway
38″ x 40″ x 15″

The artwork on this page was made from recycled bricks that people donated to me for use in my art rather than throwing them away.

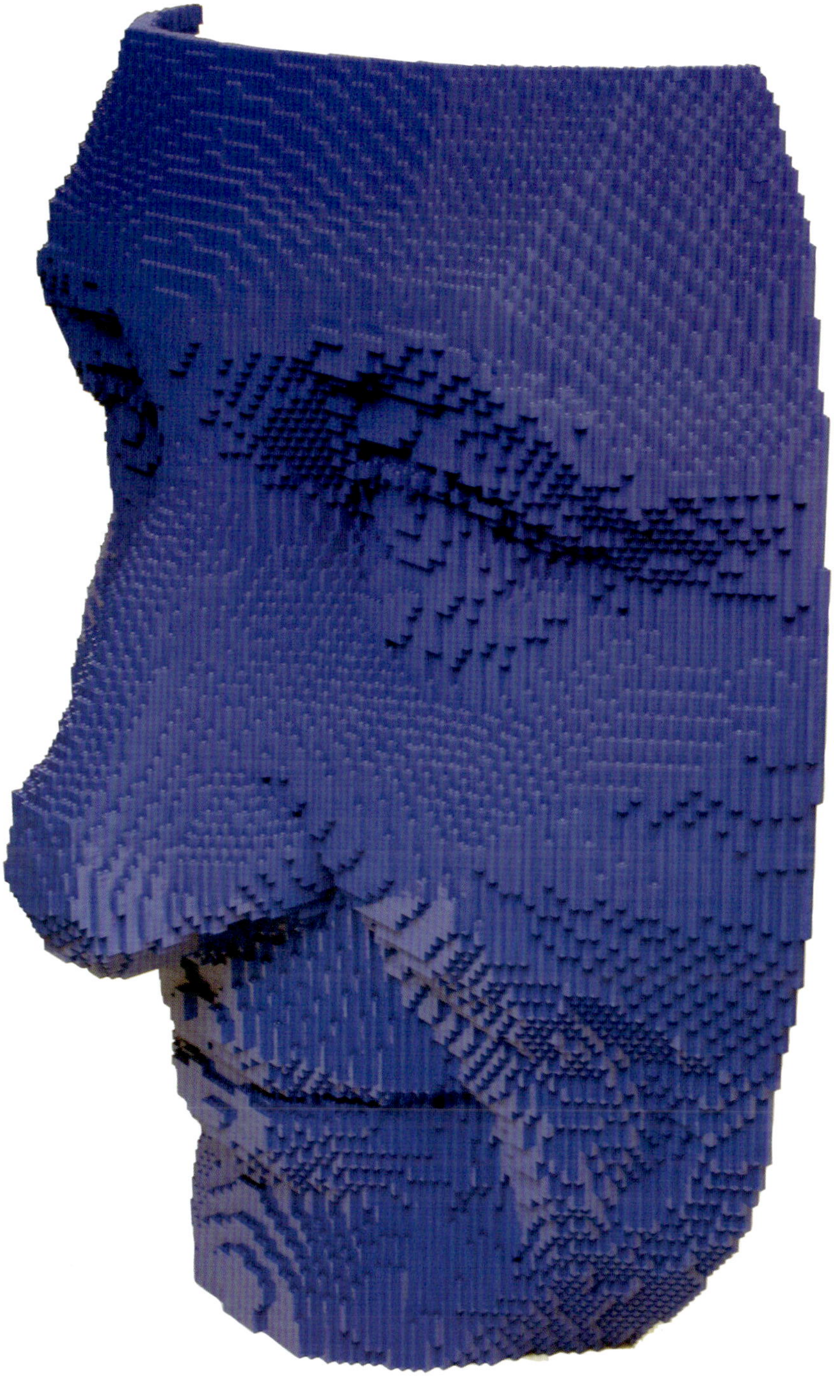

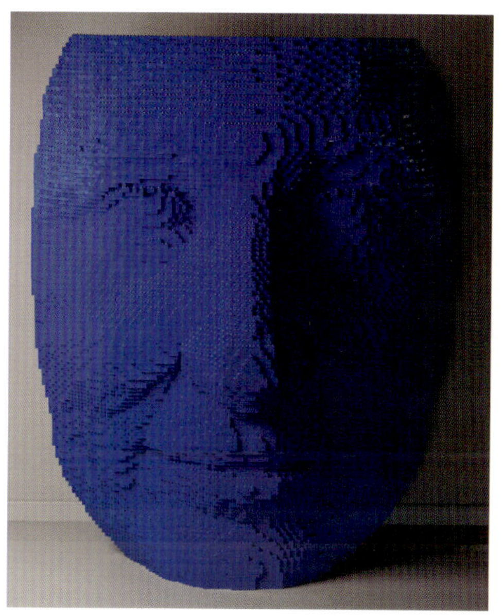

Blue Facemask
48″ x 40″ x 18″

Inside the Brick Art Studio

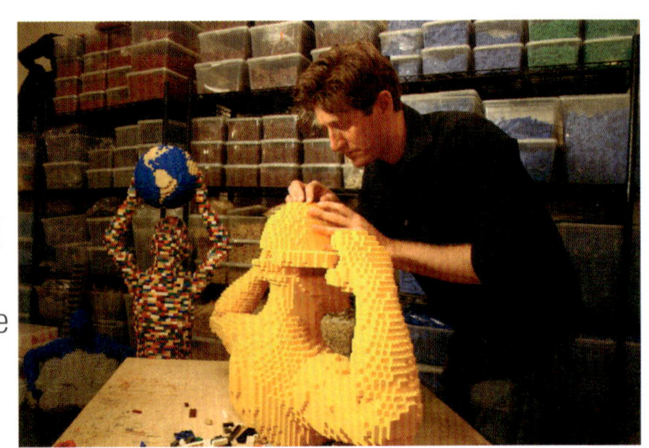

My art studio in New York City is made up of banks and banks of brick, all in rank and file order. The LEGO bricks are sorted by shape and color on tall shelves into clear bins from floor to ceiling and are organized by shade and pigment so that walking into my studio is a little like walking into a glow of a rainbow.

As you know, LEGO bricks snap together very well, but when I am creating a sculpture, there is more to the process than just clicking bricks. Everything starts with inspiration and an idea. Inspiration can come from anywhere, but I try and draw on my own experiences and emotions. Once I am inspired, I try to picture in my mind what the sculpture is going to look like when it is finished. I want to have a good vision of the sculpture before I put down that first brick.

So, because I only have a picture of the finished art in my mind - I do a lot of sketching in my studio (and on planes and restaurant napkins too). The studio is always stocked with plenty of 'Brickpaper' which is sort of like graph paper, but instead of having little squares, it has little rectangles that are the shape of the bricks. It is on this paper that the image in my mind becomes a blueprint for construction.

Once I start building, I glue the bricks together. Although the LEGO bricks would stay together just fine, I want to make sure the sculptures are permanently put together when they are shipped around the world. I find art gallery folks get grumpy when they open a box that is supposed to contain a sculpture and all they find is a bunch of loose bricks (and a note that says 'some assembly required'). On those rare occasions when I actually make a mistake after gluing the bricks together, a pair of pliers and a chisel are sometimes necessary.

Also in the studio, I tend to collect my favorite candies. It keeps me going on those extra big creations, and tends to lend a little inspiration along the way!

Portraits

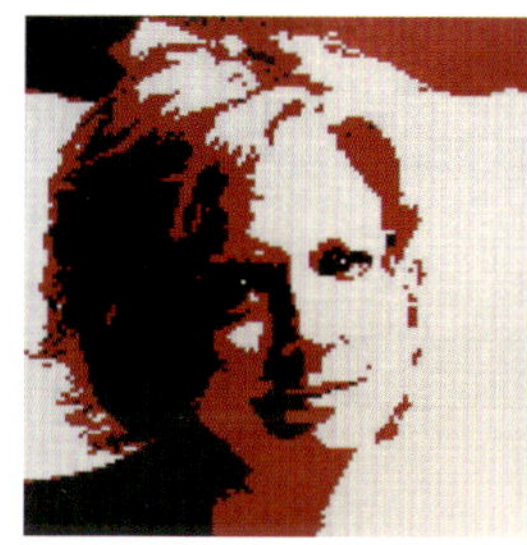 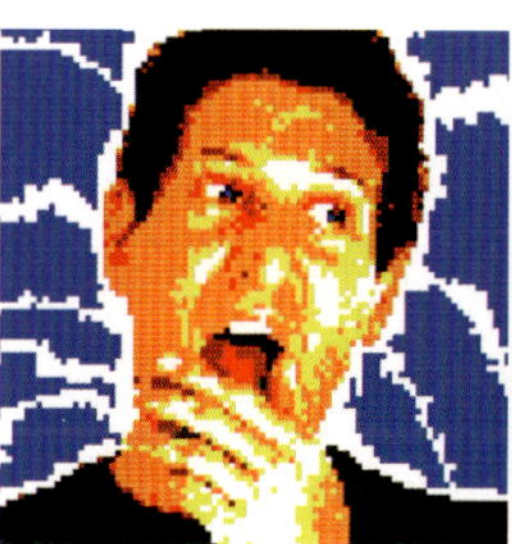 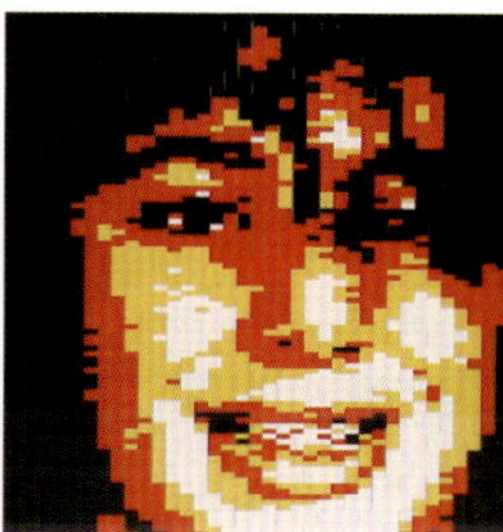 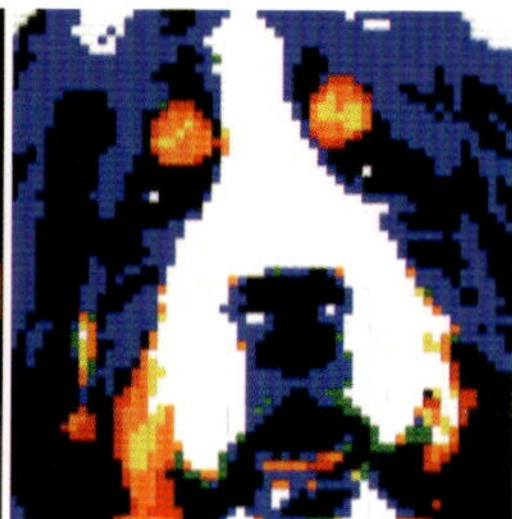

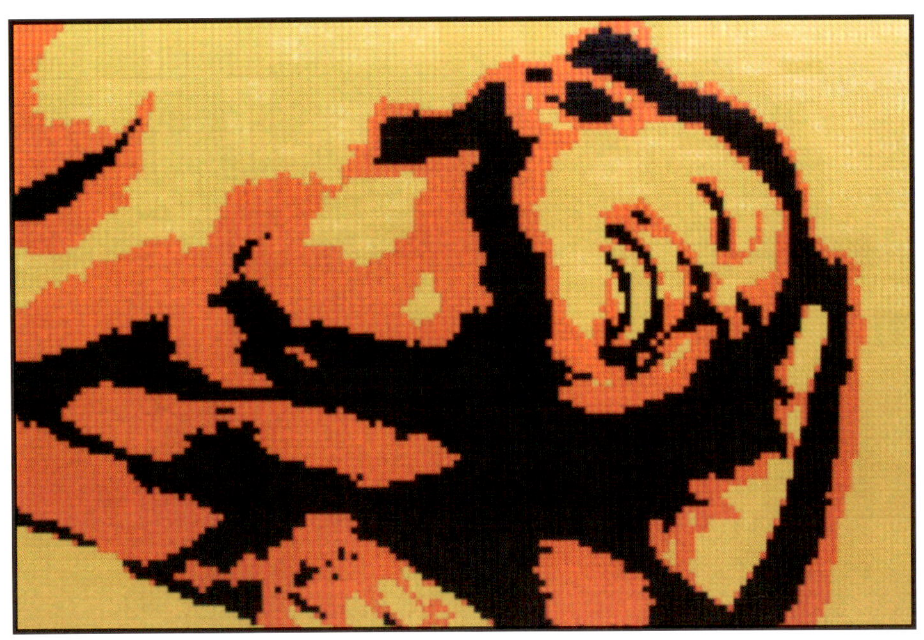

Courtney Yellow
30″ x 45″

Untitled
32″ x 32″

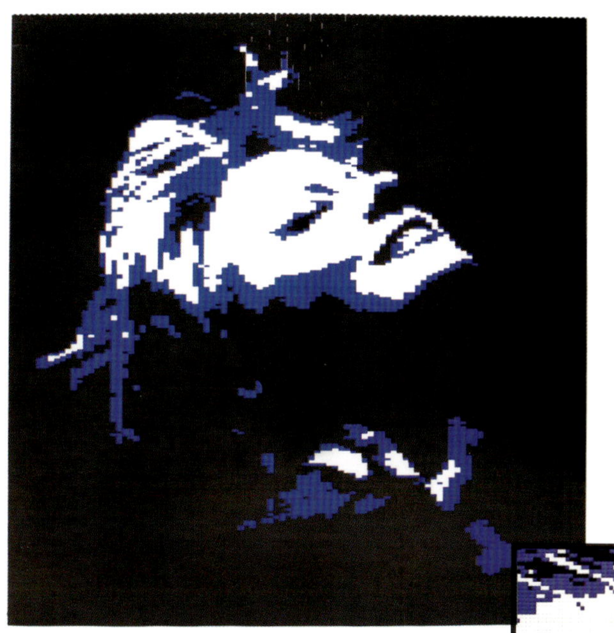

Untitled
45" x 45"

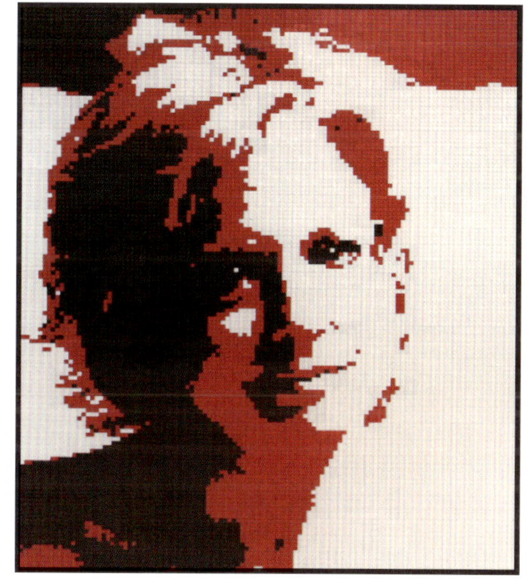

Untitled
36" x 45"

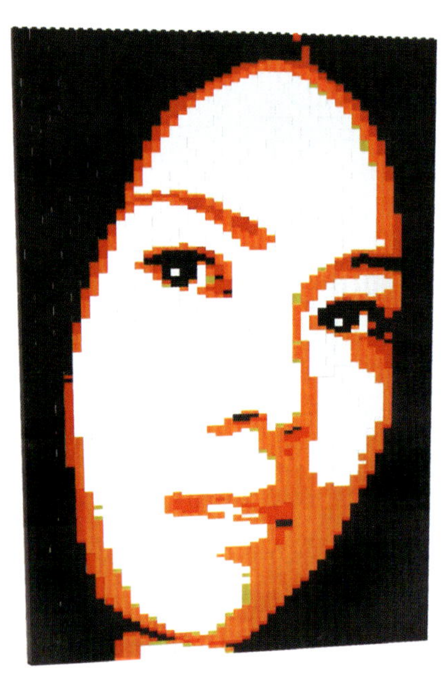

Untitled
18″x 24″

Cute Kid
20" x 26"

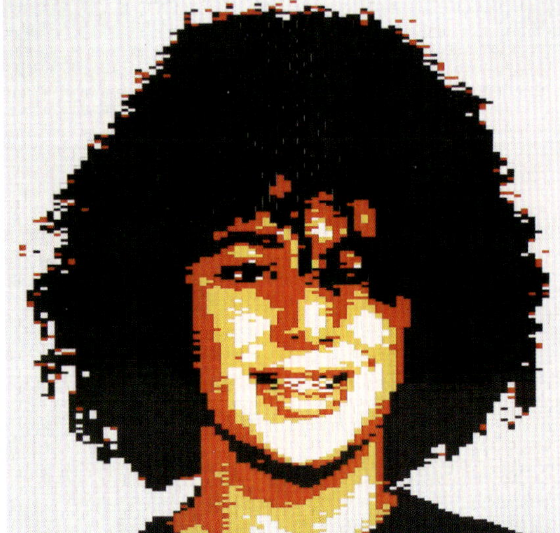

Eric
25" x 25"

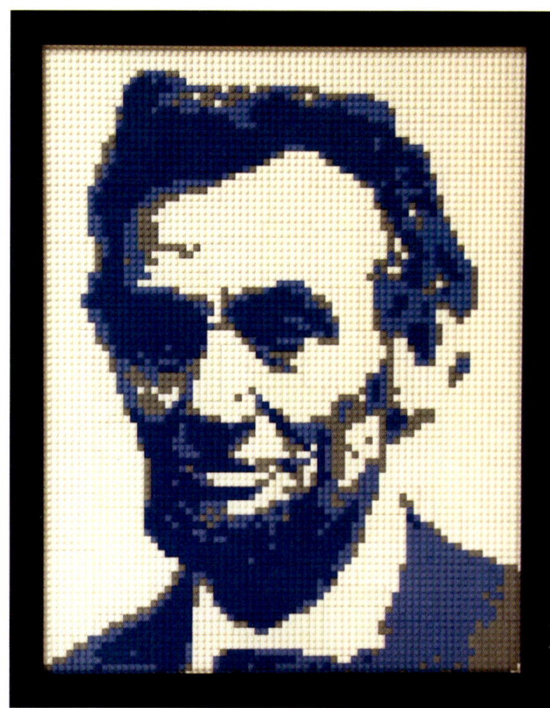

Lincoln
28" x 22"

Since Lincoln governed during the Civil War, it seemed only appropriate that I create a portrait of both blue and gray. I have a lot of extra blue and gray.

Shocking Self Portrait
28" x 22"

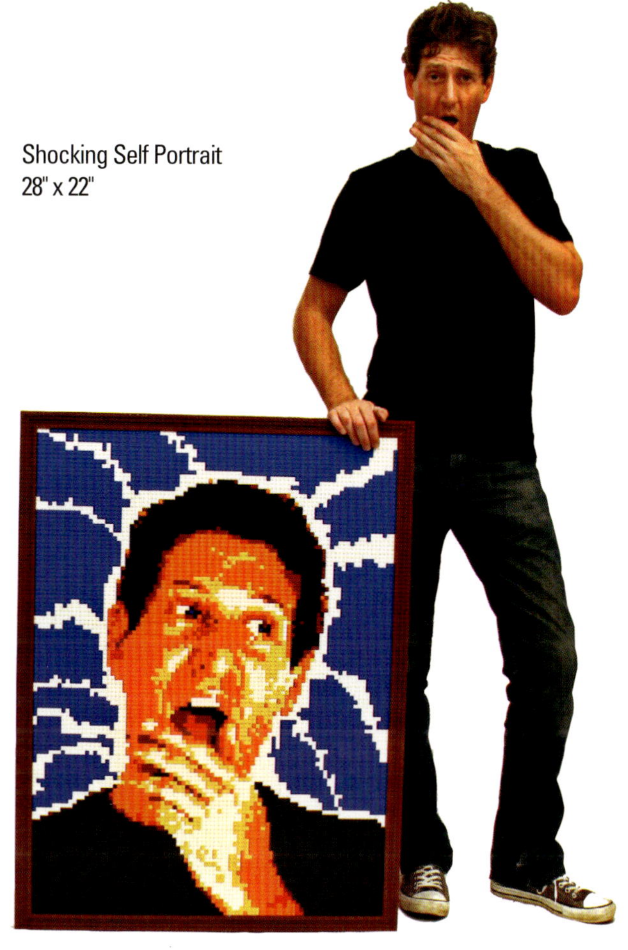

Lonely Night
60" x 9"

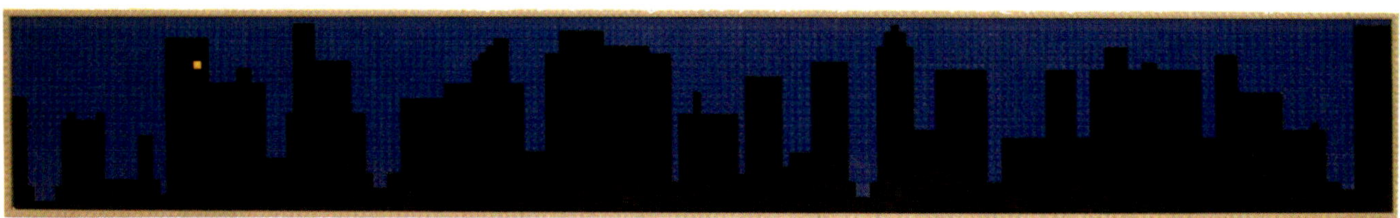

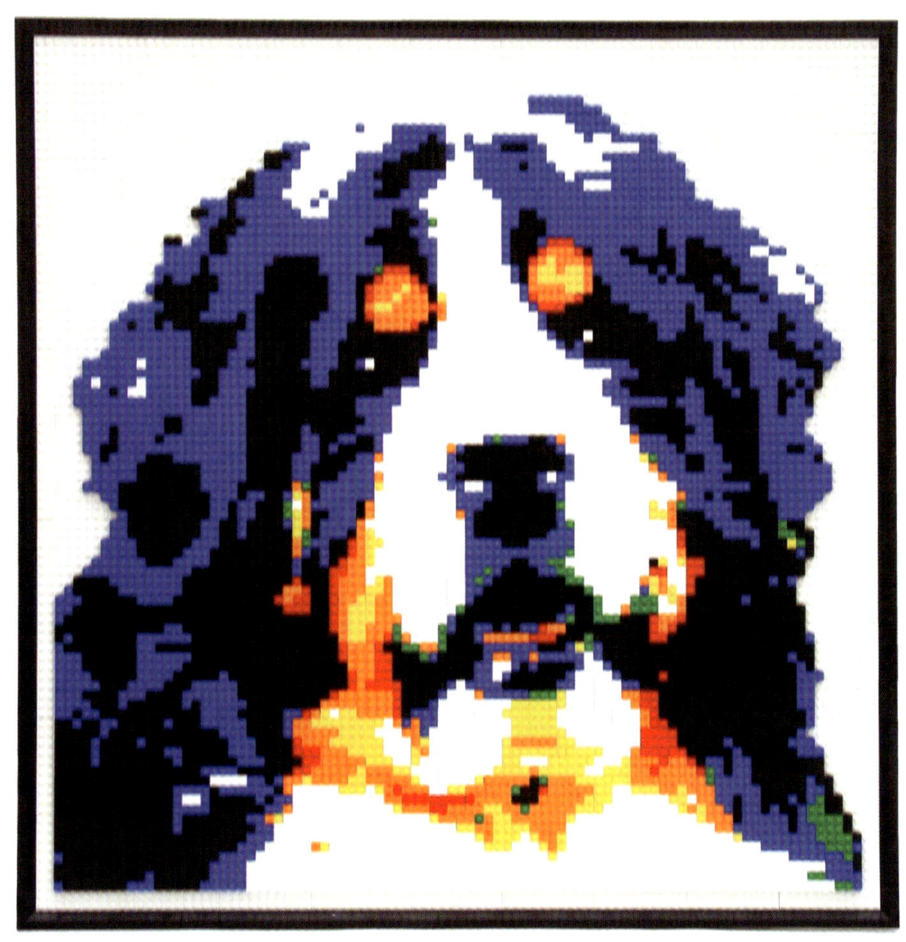

Jack the Dog
30" x 30"

Jack is a Bernese Mountain dog. Bernese Mountain dogs are working dogs with origins in the farm areas of Switzerland. Switzerland is a country that remains neutral. Neutral is the gear I thought my father's car was in when I stepped on the gas and slammed it into the garage door. The Doors sang a song called "Light My Fire." Fire is how I lost the feeling in my right index finger. Finger licking good is how I like my chicken. Chicken was my unfortunate nickname when I played soccer. Soccer was the only intramural sport I played in college. College is where I found out that I don't know jack. Jack is a Bernese Mountain dog.

Self Portrait
27″ x 36″ x 3″

Built using my childhood bricks that are over 25 years old.

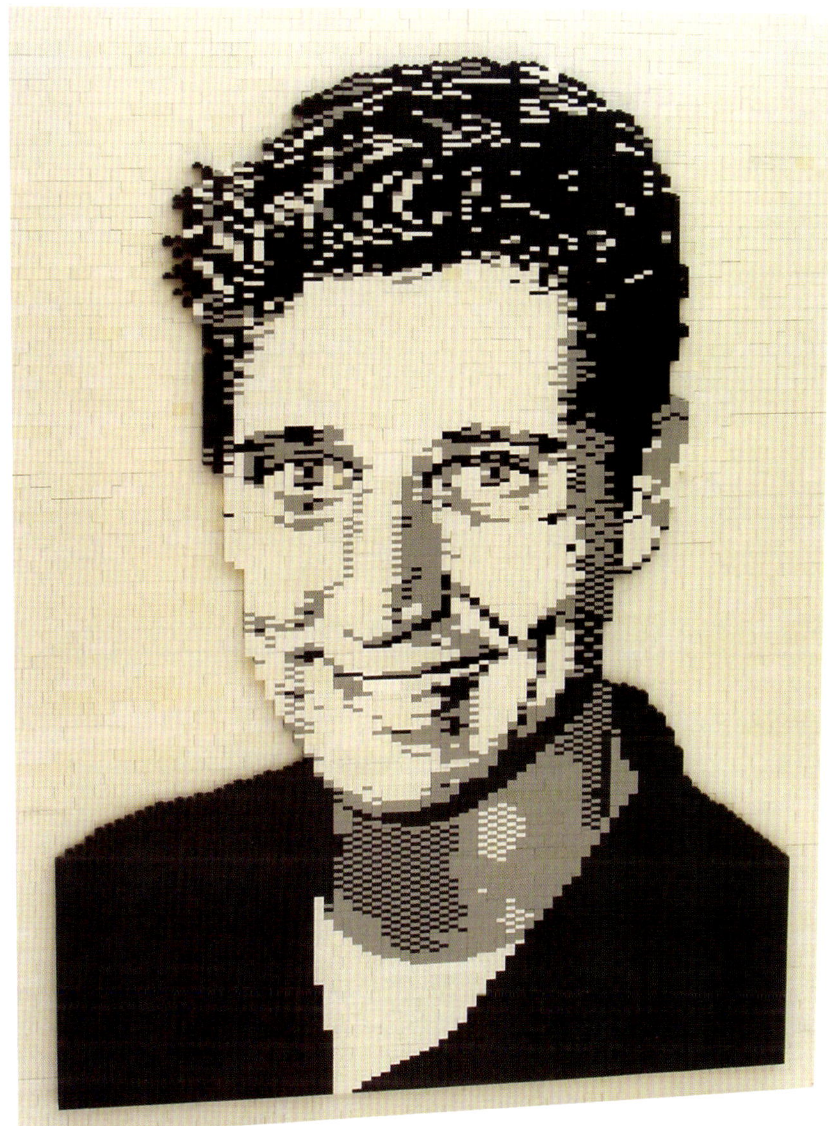

From My Brickspective

1. LEGO can take you anywhere.
I started doing large scale sculptures out of LEGO bricks about ten years ago. I had sculpted with more traditional media, but I wanted to explore using a toy from my childhood as an art medium. The sculptures got a pretty good response from friends and family, so I put photos of them up on my website, brickartist.com. Soon after, I was getting commissions from folks around the world. Within a few years, I was a full time LEGO artist. Since then, I have put together museum exhibitions and gallery shows all over the globe. I have been asked to send sculptures to Hong Kong, Dubai, Paris, London, Singapore, even Kansas City. I never dreamed that creating with LEGO would take me to places like Hawaii, Stockholm or Appleton, Wisconsin, or even as a guest on the *The Colbert Report* and *Mythbusters*. I got to design a LEGO room on *Extreme Makeover: Home Edition*. And weirdest of all, my LEGO artwork actually became a category on the game show, *Jeopardy!*

2. There is no cheating in LEGO.
I don't know how many times folks have come up to me and said "Are you gluing your bricks? Well that's cheating!" And I wonder to myself, "Are you the LEGO referee?" The thing is LEGO bricks hold together remarkable well. They are an amazing construction tool. But my sculptures are shipped around the world. And the shipping process can take a toll on any artwork. So to make sure my sculptures arrive in one piece, I glue them together. This is not cheating. Anything one does creatively with LEGO cannot be considered cheating. In fact, the only way there might be cheating in LEGO is if one was to use only Lincoln Logs.

3. There is nothing that cannot be built out of LEGO.
When I was a child and wanted to get a dog, my folks didn't let me, so I built myself a dog. It was multi-colored, and of course being built out of those rectangular bricks, it was a bit boxy in places. I called it a boxer. LEGO is a versatile medium. As a toy, it lets your imagination rule the day. Growing up, if I wanted to pretend to be a rock star, I could build myself a guitar. If I wanted to pretend to be an astronaut, I could build myself a khan only a toy. By using LEGO as an art medium, I have been able to put together an entire museum exhibit that is currently touring the globe. It has become a very popular exhibit as both kids and adults are attracted to the idea of artwork created solely out of LEGO. I truly believe that I can create anything out of LEGO bricks.

4. 1.5 million LEGO bricks are not enough.
The LEGO company says that there are 62 LEGO bricks for every person on the planet. That means there is a pretty big group of people who are missing some bricks all because of me. As an artist, I want to make sure I have enough bricks on hand that I can build whatever I can think of, at any time. That means I have to keep an art studio full of bricks in all shapes and colors. They are all arranged by size, and are in clear plastic bins lined up on shelves based on color. Walking into my studio is a little like walking into a rainbow. I need all those bricks because who knows what I might be creating next: a life-size human form, a replica of New Orleans, maybe even a full size boat? Just in case, my studio in New York City houses about 1.5 million bricks at any given time. And as I use the bricks up, I have to keep that inventory up to date, so I am ordering new bricks monthly. I don't know if that means there are less or more bricks for everyone on the planet.

5. The LEGO art movement has begun.
One of the most common questions people ask me is "How can I get your job?" I tell them just to go do it. I am an independent artist, and I use LEGO bricks as my art medium. Creating art is my passion. It can take weeks to create a LEGO sculpture, but I fall into an almost trance while I'm working and creating. Many of my works center on the phenomena of how everyday life, people and raw emotion are intertwined. Often my art is a reenactment of my personal feelings. I am inspired by my own experiences, emotions and the journeys I am taking. Many people write to me and tell me they are going to become LEGO artists themselves. They send me photos of their sculptures and creations. It looks to me like a new art movement has begun. I call it the LEGO art movement, and don't be surprised if five or ten years from now they will be teaching it in art classes.

Novelty

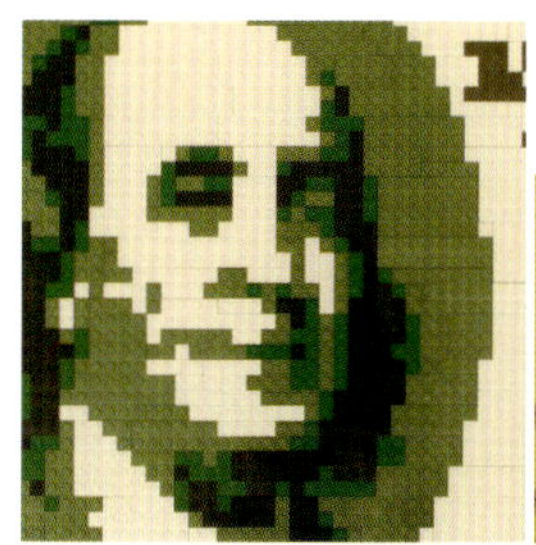
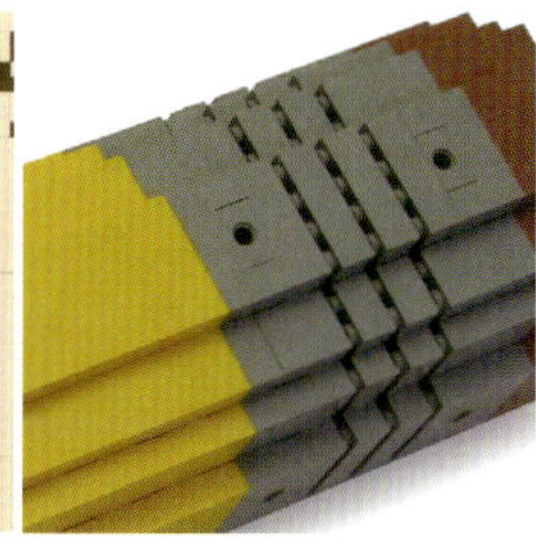
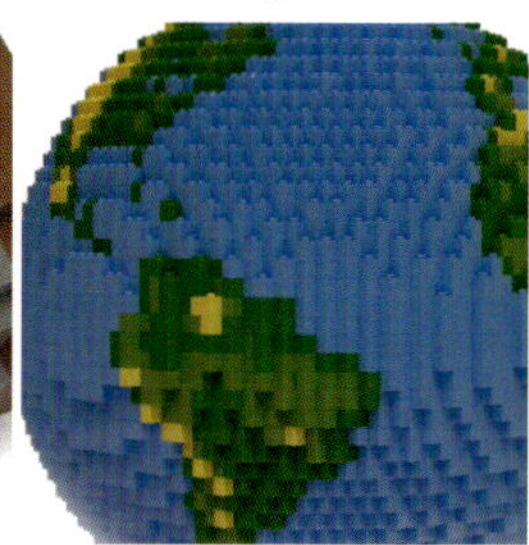
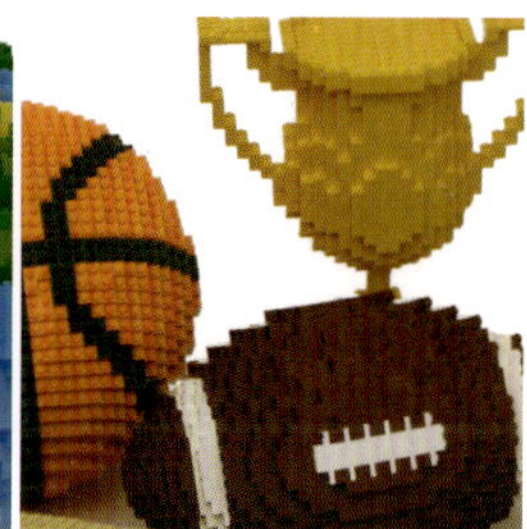

Cello
18"x 55" x 11"

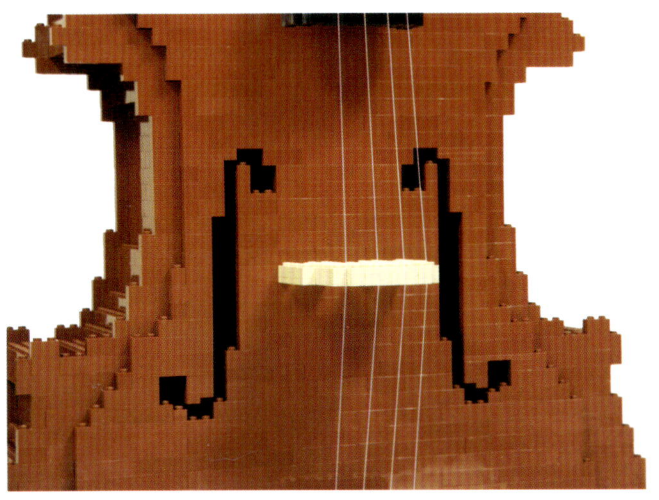

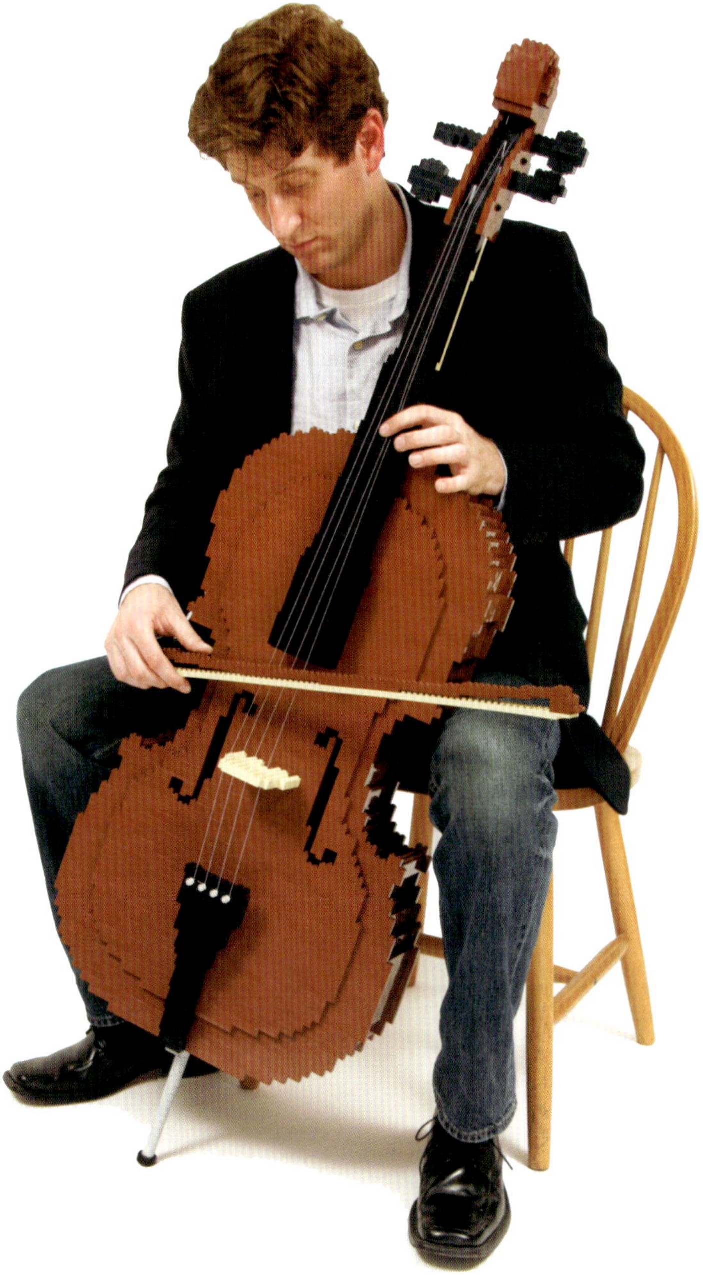

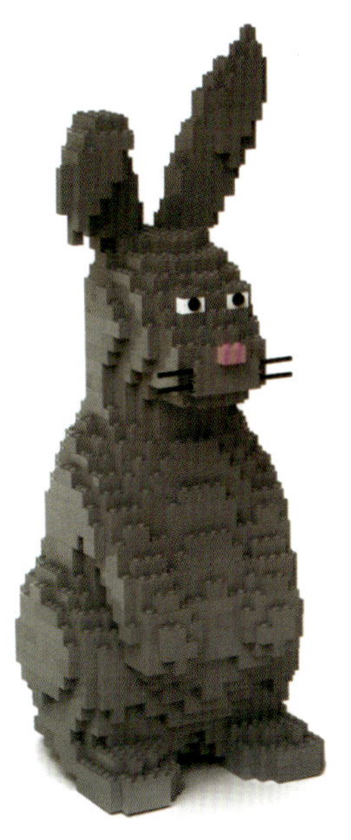

Capcom Robot
46" x 54" x 28"

The Robot was based on a character from Capcom's video game, Lost Planet. Although I looked at a lot of pictures of the robot, I never actually played the game.

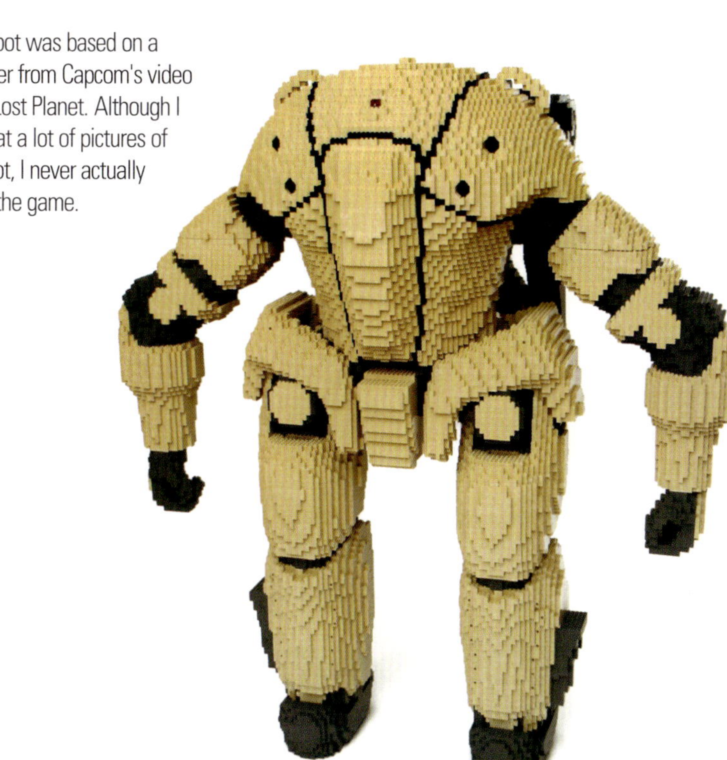

Speedboat
30" x 121" x 48"

The boat is a replica of a Chris-Craft Speedster that I built at the Seattle Boat Show. I used almost a quarter of a million bricks over ten days to build the boat.

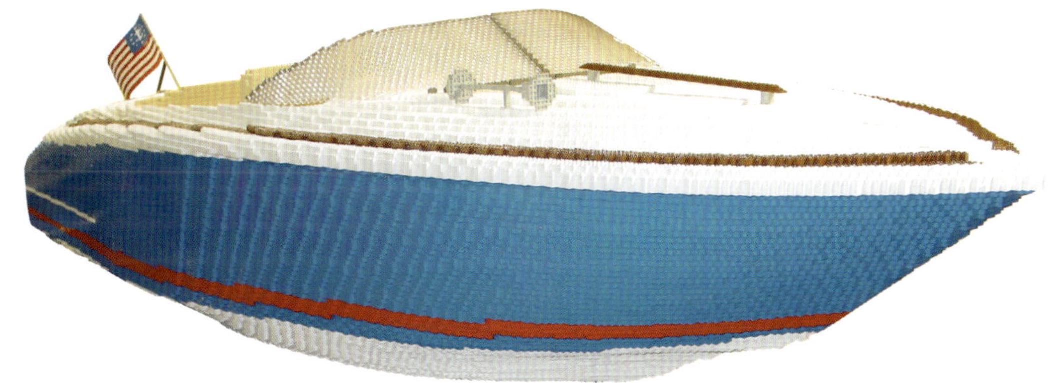

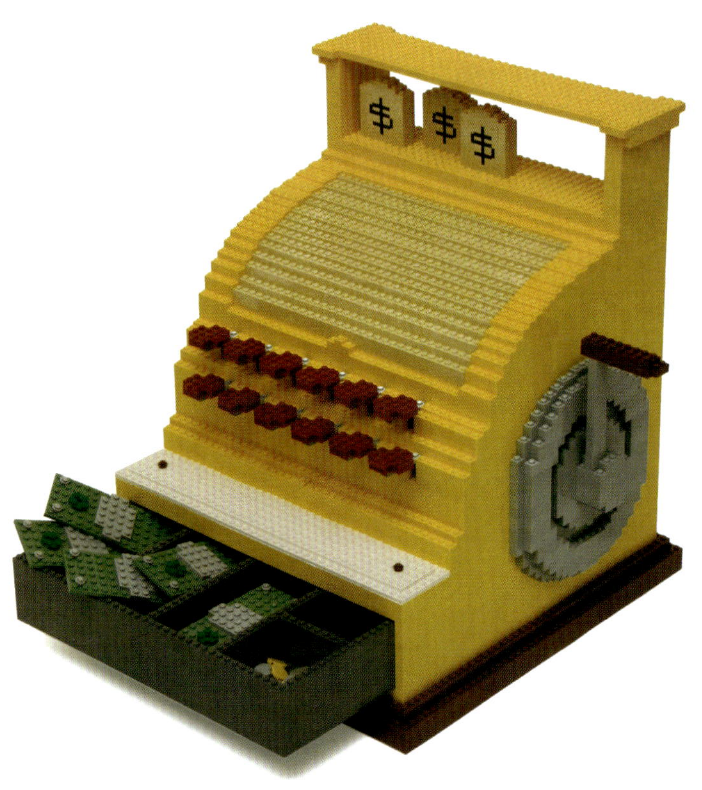

Old Fashioned Cash Register
15" x 22" x 16"

I created a yellow old fashioned cash register reminiscient of a toy cash register I had when I was a kid. I remember playing with the toy cash register, pretending I was a store clerk and ringing up imaginary customers. They never had the right amount of cash and I always found myself giving them imaginary change. Then one day my imaginary manager told me my cash drawer came up eighteen imaginary dollars short. He said I needed to reimburse him for the missing imaginary $18 or he'd have to let me go. I handed him an imaginary twenty, but he said that there was nothing in my hand and I should stop wasting his time. I told him that I didn't have any other imaginary money, and I didn't want his imaginary attitude.

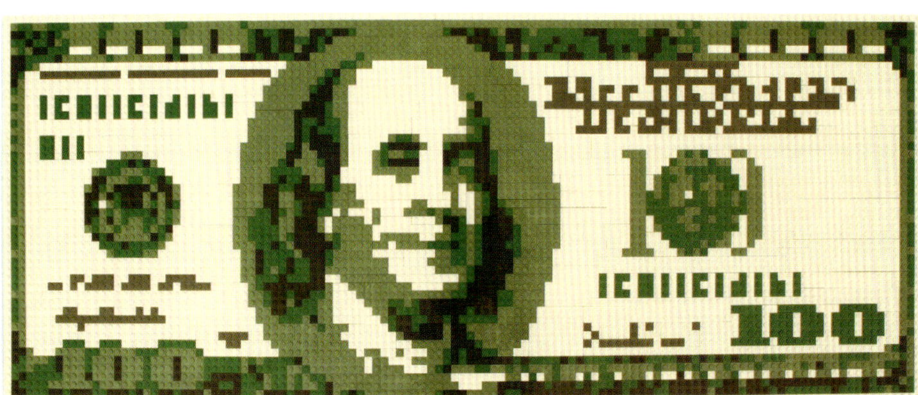

Dollar Bill
38" x 15"

Stubby Pencil
16" x 5" x 5"

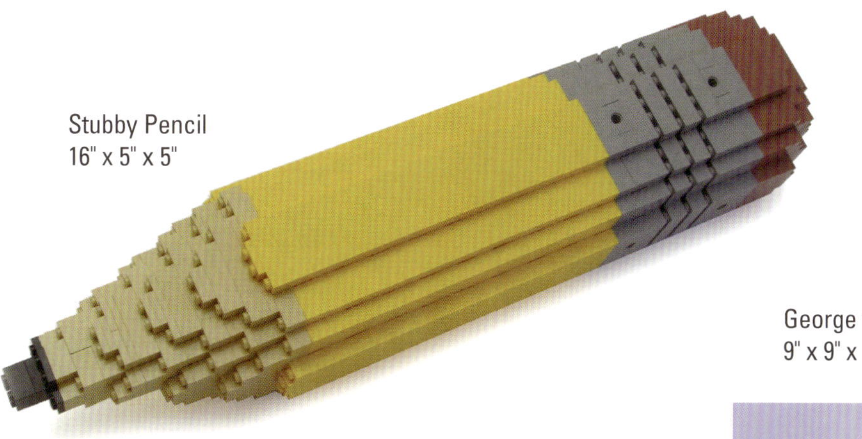

George the Monkey
9" x 9" x 12"

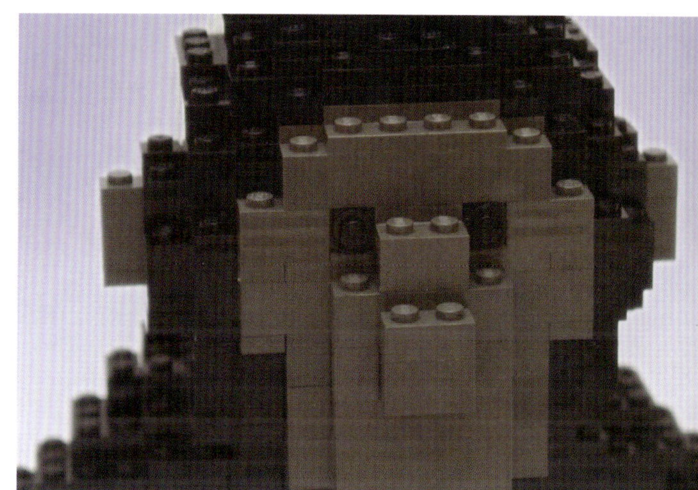

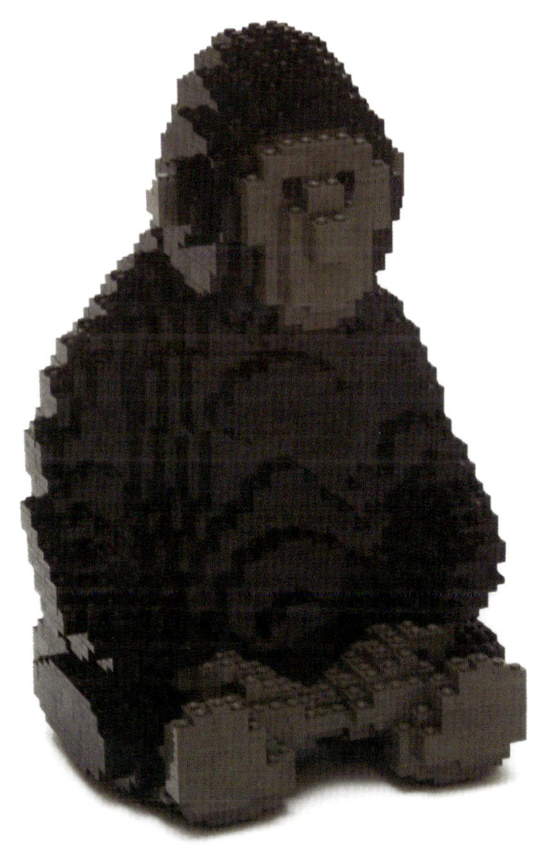

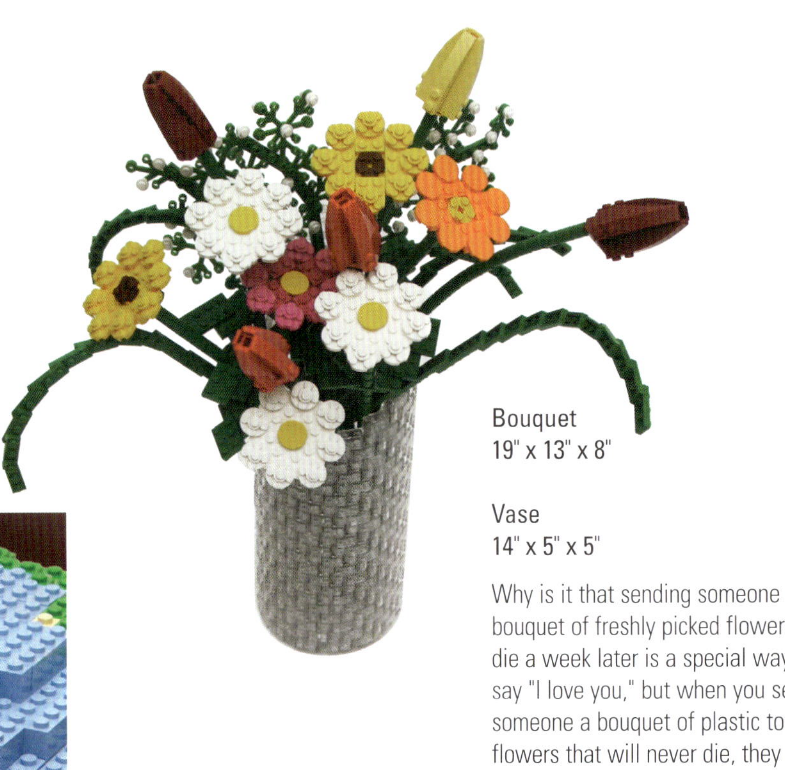

Bouquet
19" x 13" x 8"

Vase
14" x 5" x 5"

Why is it that sending someone a bouquet of freshly picked flowers that die a week later is a special way to say "I love you," but when you send someone a bouquet of plastic toy flowers that will never die, they think you should get out more?

Globe
15″ x 17″ x 15″

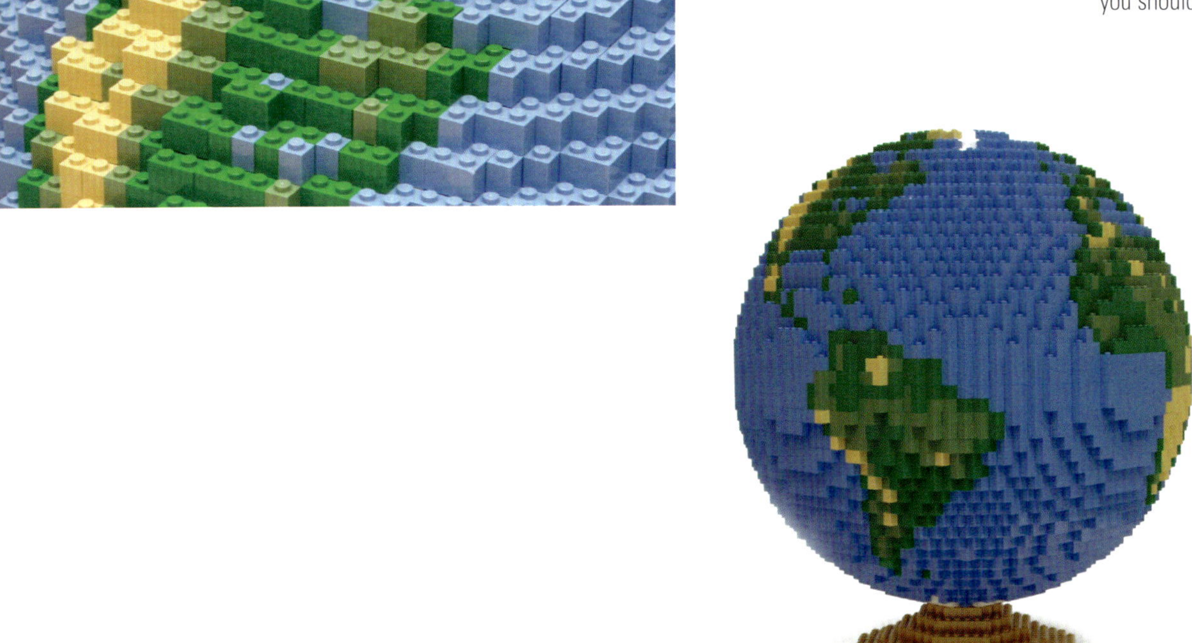

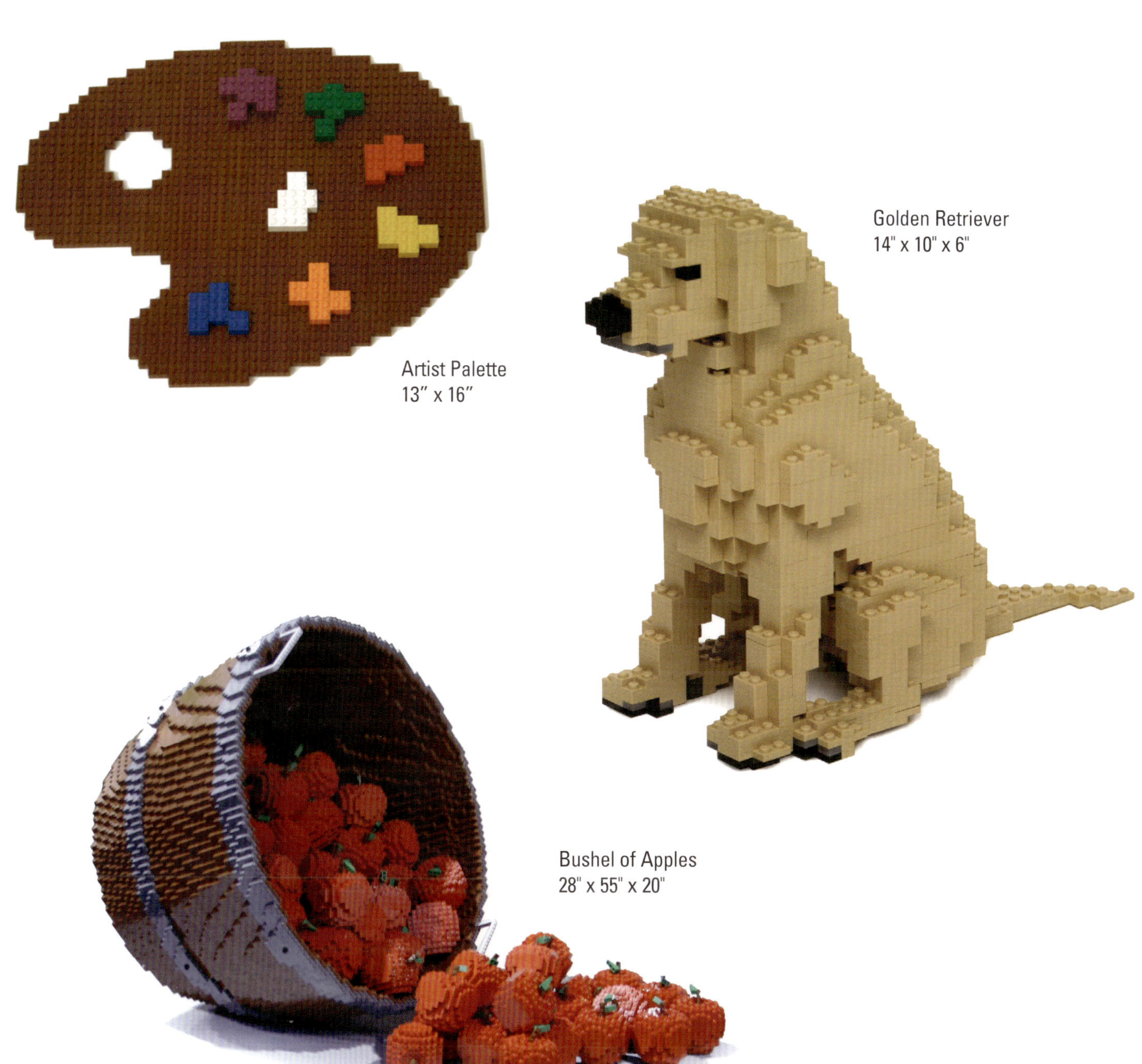

Artist Palette
13″ x 16″

Golden Retriever
14" x 10" x 6"

Bushel of Apples
28" x 55" x 20"

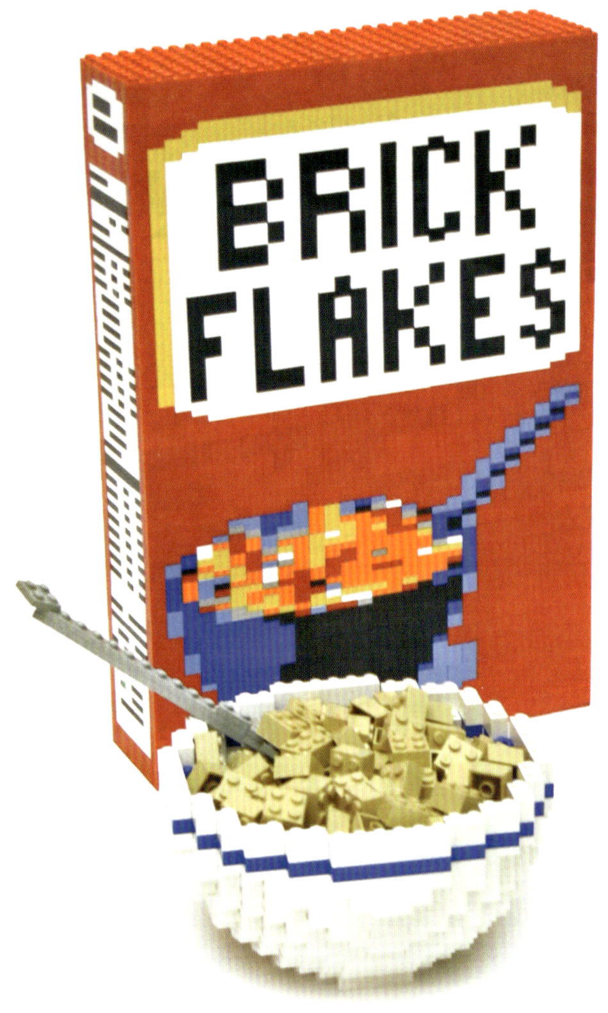

Breakfast
Cereal Box: 9" x 13" x 3"
Bowl: 6" x 4" x 6"

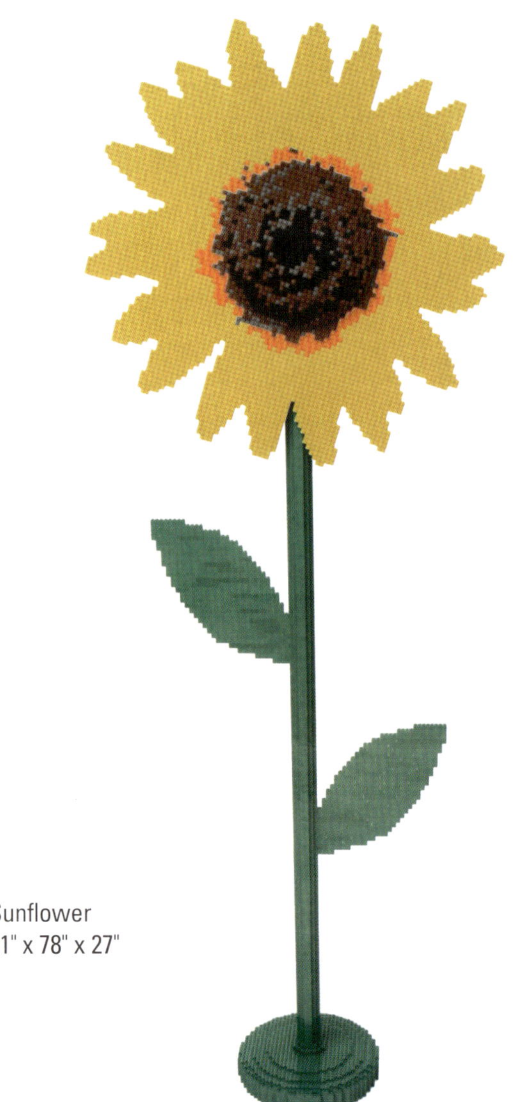

Sunflower
11" x 78" x 27"

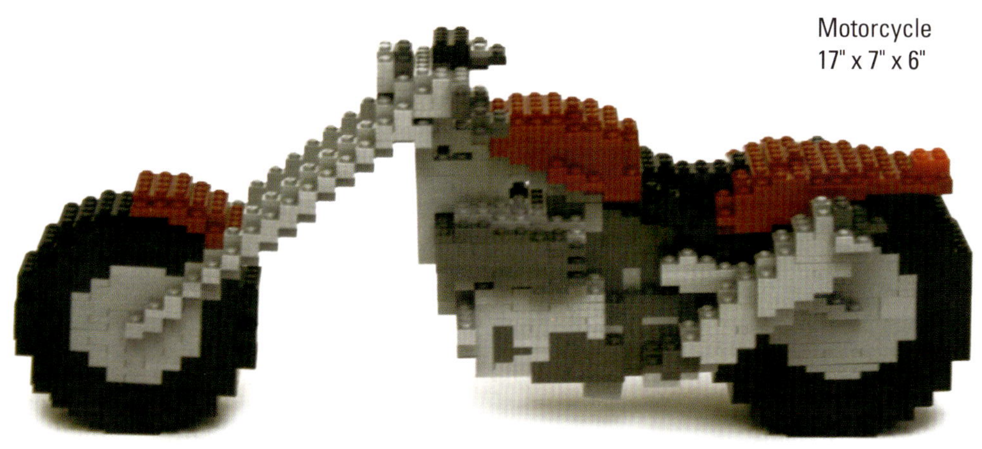

Motorcycle
17" x 7" x 6"

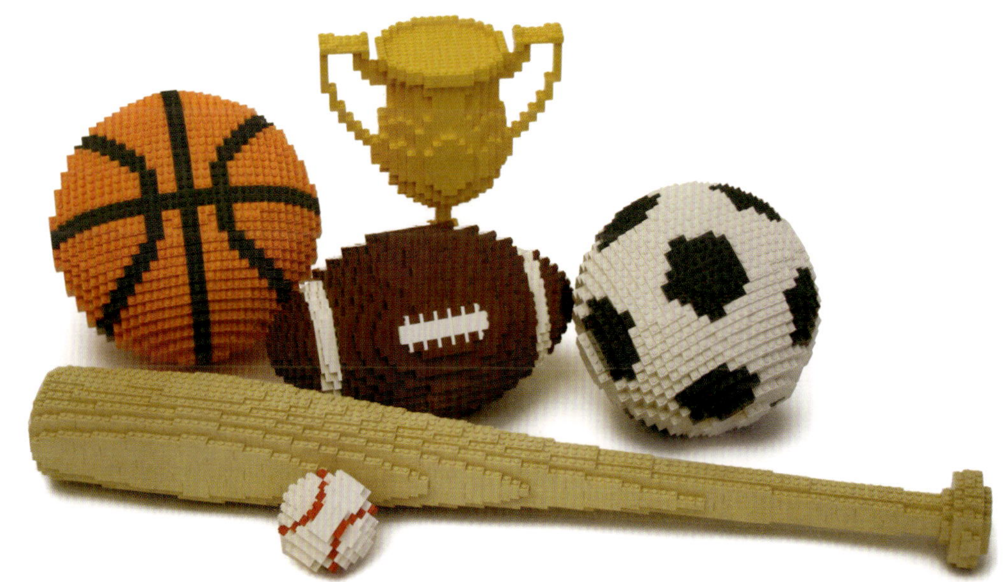

Sports Equipment

Football: 12" x 7" x 7"
Basketball: 10" x 10" x 10"
Baseball: 3.5" x 3.5" x 3.5"
Bat: 34" x 5" x 5"
Soccerball: 9" x 9" x 9"
Trophy: 11" x 10" x 7"

Artist Statement

When I was a lawyer I quickly came to realize I was more comfortable sitting on the floor creating sculptures than I was sitting in a boardroom negotiating contracts. My personal search for overall happiness paved the way to becoming a full-time working artist. However, it can't be said that my experience as a lawyer has not influenced my work as an artist; in fact, some might say it has defined me.

Creating art is my passion. Many of my works center on the phenomena of how everyday life, people and raw emotion are intertwined. Often my art is a reenactment of my personal feelings. I am inspired by my own experiences, emotions and the journeys I am taking.

The primary medium for my work is LEGO plastic bricks. I use this as a medium because I enjoy seeing people's reactions to artwork created from something with which they are familiar. Everyone can relate to it since it is a toy that many children have at home. I want to elevate this simple plaything to a place it has never been before. I also appreciate the cleanliness of the medium. The right angles. The distinct lines. As so often in life, it is a matter of perspective. Up close, the shape of the brick is distinctive. But from a distance, those right angles and distinct lines change to curves. It takes weeks to complete a life size human form. The long hours of creating a new piece bring me immense satisfaction. When I am working on a project I enjoy, I completely submerge myself into the project, going into a trance-like state.

On and off, I intentionally intermix subject matter that is steeped in heavy sentiment with the lighthearted and whimsical. The purpose of this is two-fold. I realize families and children are drawn to my art because of the unique medium in which it was created and I welcome that. But it is also a necessary break for me to create whimsy in addition to the construction of the complex human forms. I want to provide a break for the viewer's eye, as well as a respite for my brain.

Currently, my favorite subject is the human form. I use the male human form to represent the everyman, society, you and me. A lot of my work suggests a figure in transition. It represents the metamorphoses I am experiencing in my own life. My pieces grow out of my fears and accomplishments, as a lawyer and as an artist, as a boy and as a man. The names I give my pieces are generally unsophisticated in nature by design. I purposefully use simple titles to avoid influencing the viewer's own interpretation of the work. This stems from both my desire for the audience to have a role in the interpretation and my insecurity of defining that role for them.

The fundamental purpose to my art is to captivate people for as long as I can keep their attention. I strive to create artwork that is interesting and that is unlike anything they have seen before.

Large Sculptures

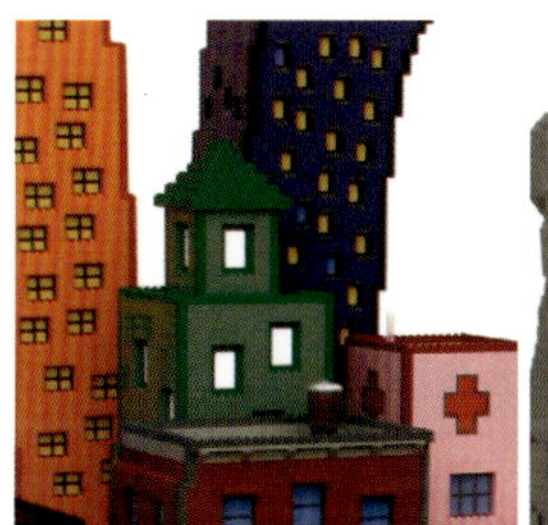

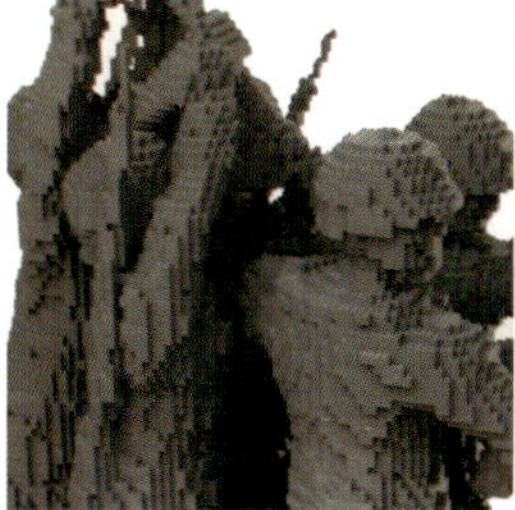

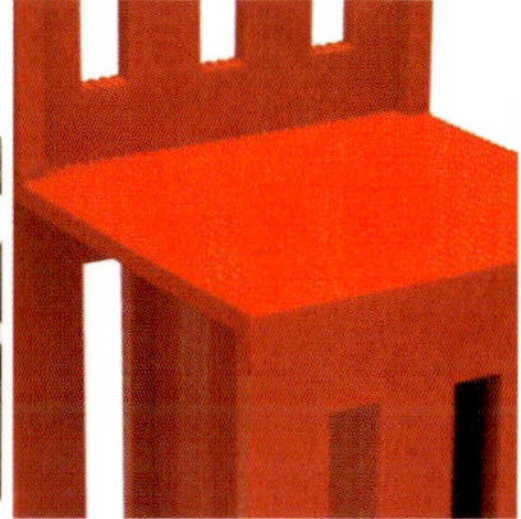

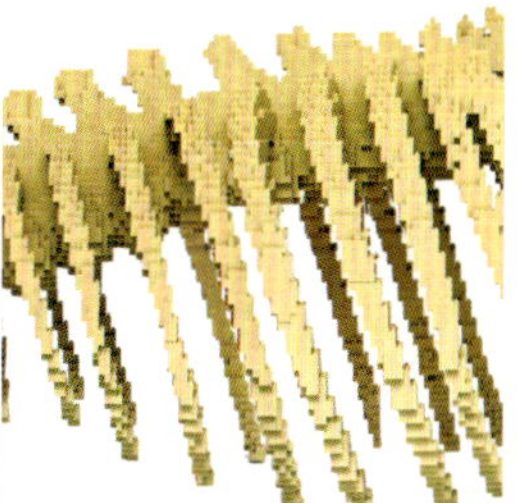

This is a poem
About a girl in a boat,
Who kept sailing around
The confines of a moat.

The moat went around
A very big palace
Inside lived a prince,
And his maid Alice.

The prince had no problems.
His life was pure pleasure.
But his love for that girl,
He could not measure.

And the girl loved him back.
Their love had been bound.
But she still sailed on her boat.
Around and around.

She didn't dare stop
For around the moat's edge
Were sharp jagged rocks
Where her boat could not wedge.

The prince watched her each day,
And watched her each night.
They'd talk all the time.
But it just wasn't right.

He begged her to jump.
And leave the boat far below.
But she kept sailing around,
Not ready to go.

"I'll catch you," he promised.
There will be no harm."
And she wanted to go
And live in his arms.

But the boat seemed so safe.
And the jump seemed so big.
She could not just leave,
And abandon her rig.

"Finally," the prince said,
As he jumped on her boat.
"If you won't come to me,
Then I'll sail on the moat!"

And they sailed on her boat,
Just watching the palace.
But they could not go back,
'Cuz it was now owned by Alice.

The moral of the story,
If you must know:
If you stay where you are,
Then you may never go.

So if one would jump,
And prepare for the hassle,
One day they will find,
They can live in the castle.

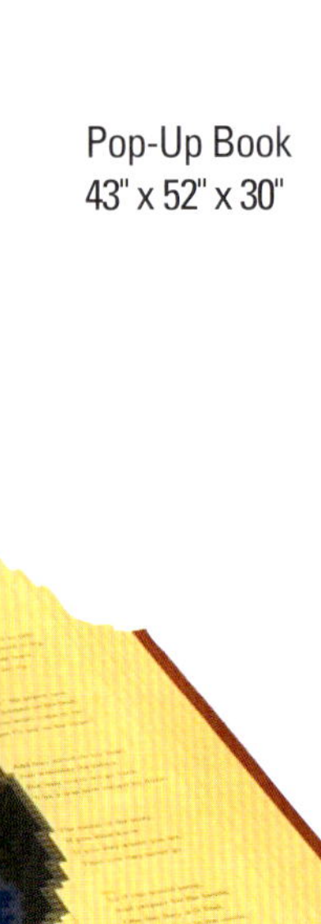

Pop-Up Book
43" x 52" x 30"

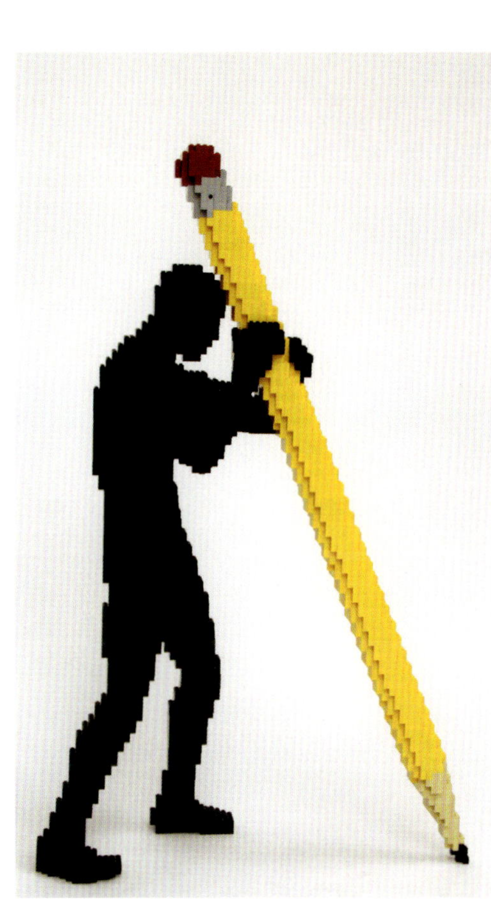

Untitled
11" x 37" x 25"

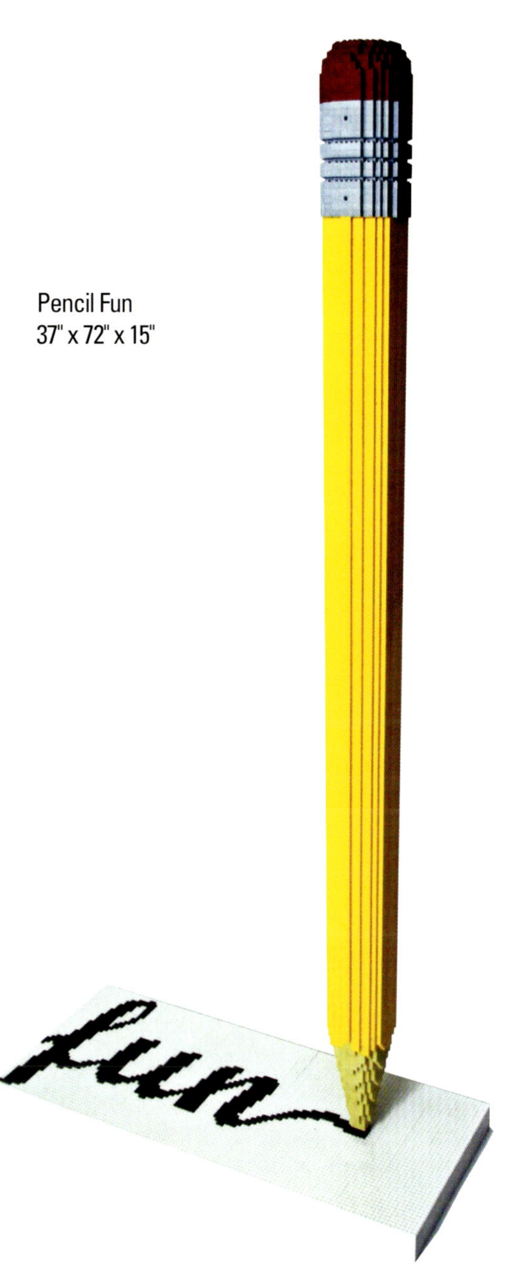

Pencil Fun
37" x 72" x 15"

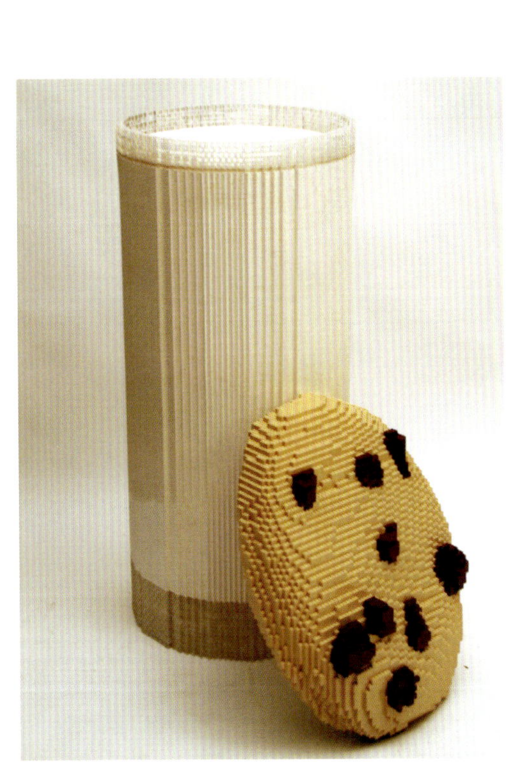

Milk & Cookie
34" x 48" x 22"

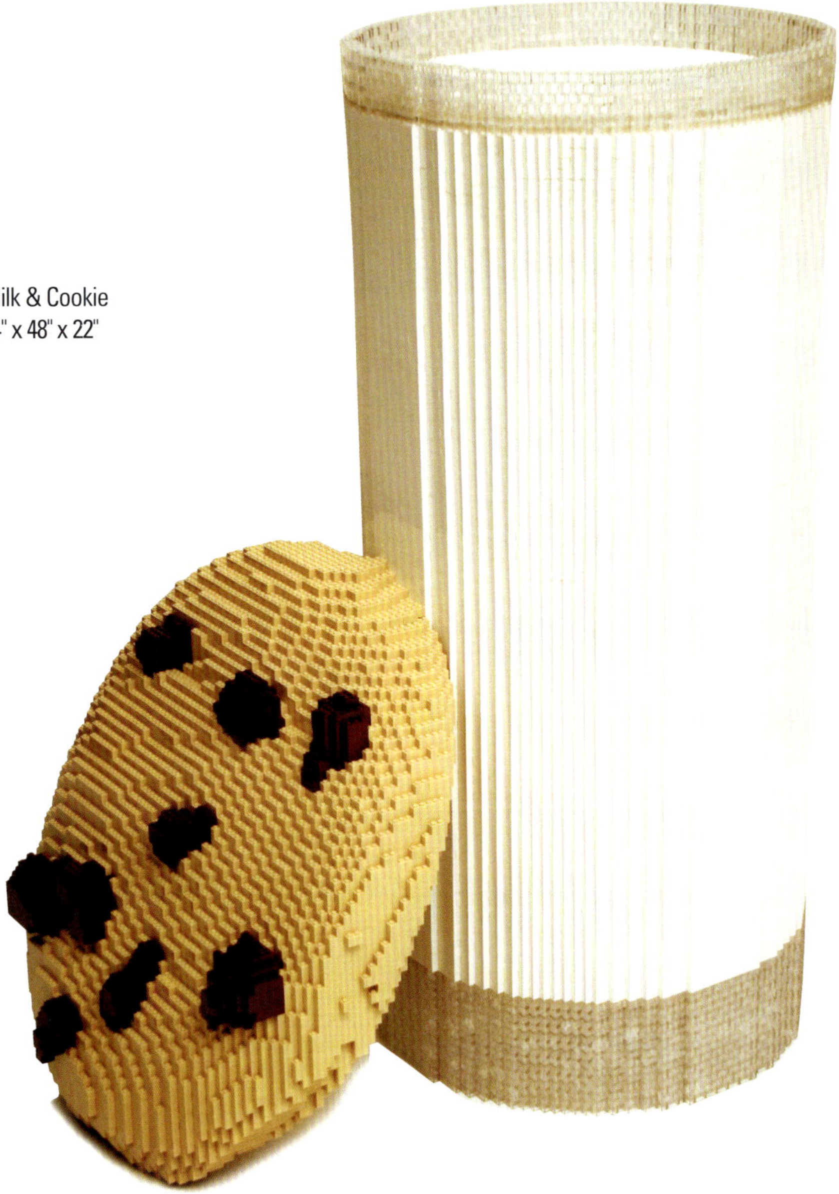

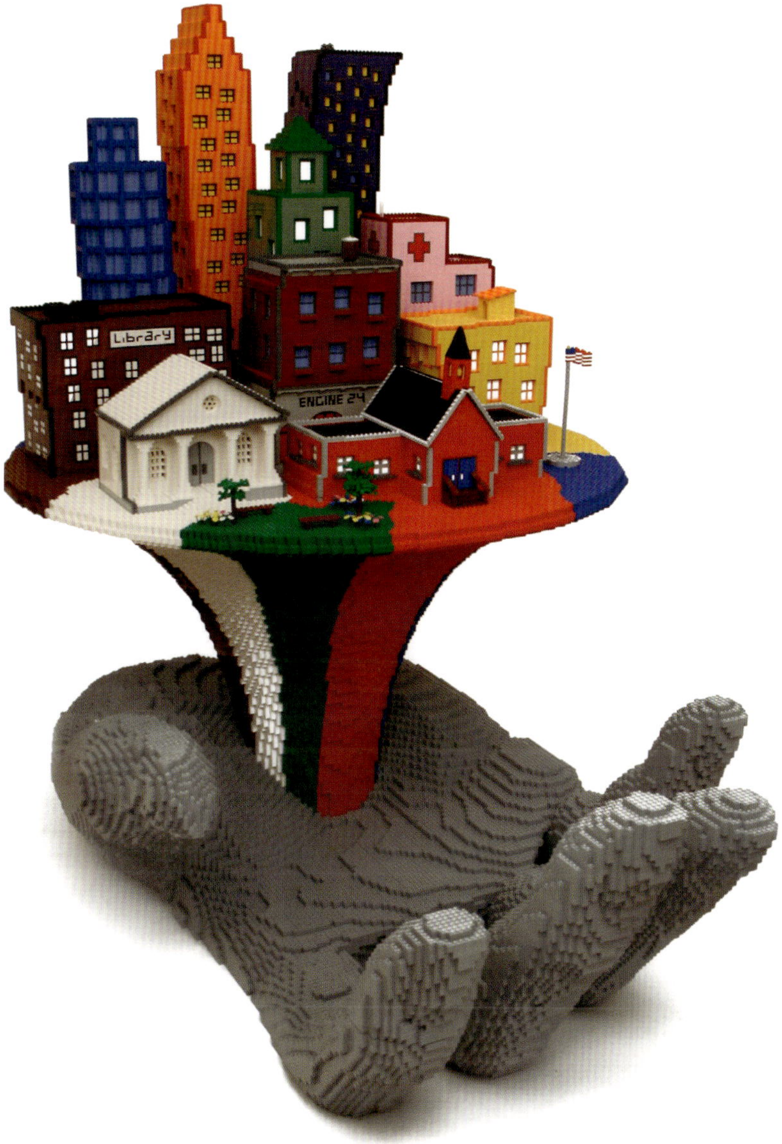

Rebirth of New Orleans
66" x 42" x 64"

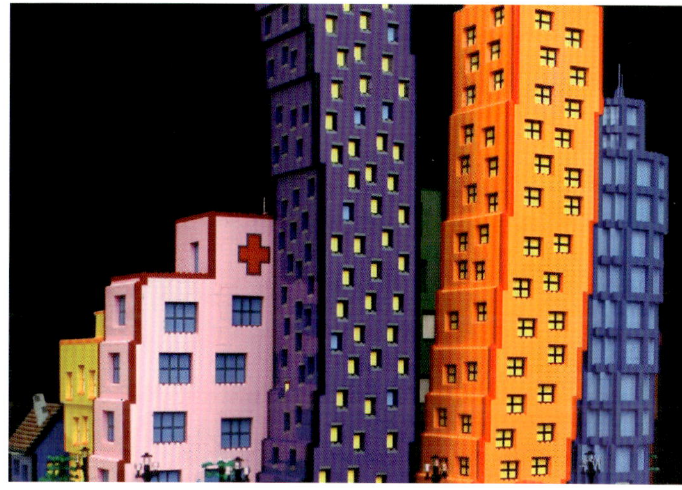

The "Rebirth of New Orleans" was commissioned in 2006 to be a permanent art display at the New Orleans Public Library. The sculpture was inspired by drawings of children. The buildings are "literal" interpretations of the drawings, hence the crooked walls, bright colors and unaligned windows. The sculpture took approximately five weeks to build and used almost 120,000 bricks.

Pluto, the Black Cat
22″ x 31″ x 19″

Ways that I am like a cat:

- We both like to drink milk.
- We both like to eat fish.
- We both like to sleep a lot.
- We both do our best work at night.
- We both believe that licking our body hair is a sufficient way to cleanse oneself.
- We both hate leashes. (Not exactly true for me.)
- We both drive poorly.

Pedestal
15" x 15" x 39"

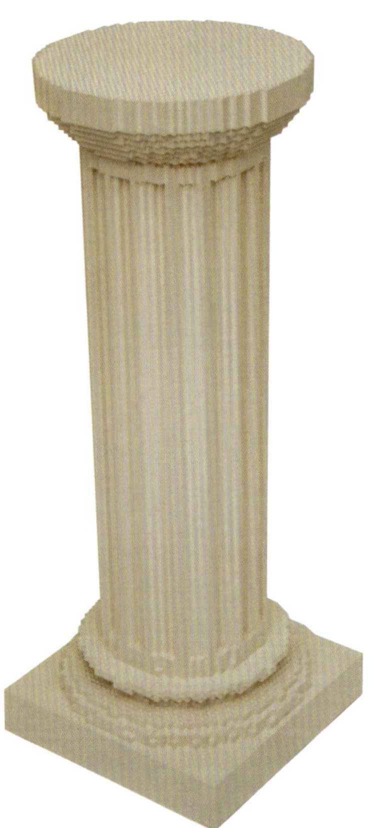

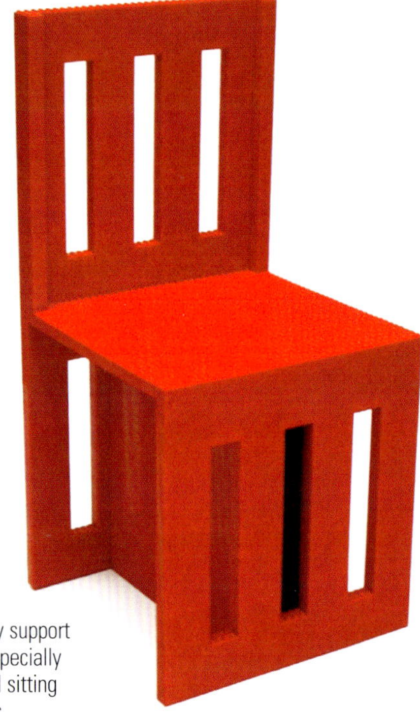

Chair
12" x 23" x 12"

This chair will actually support a full grown adult. Especially one who doesn't mind sitting on hundreds of bumps.

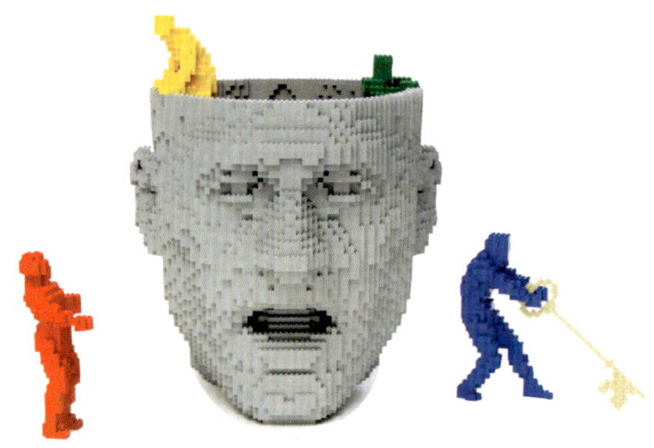

Think
42" x 26" x 22"

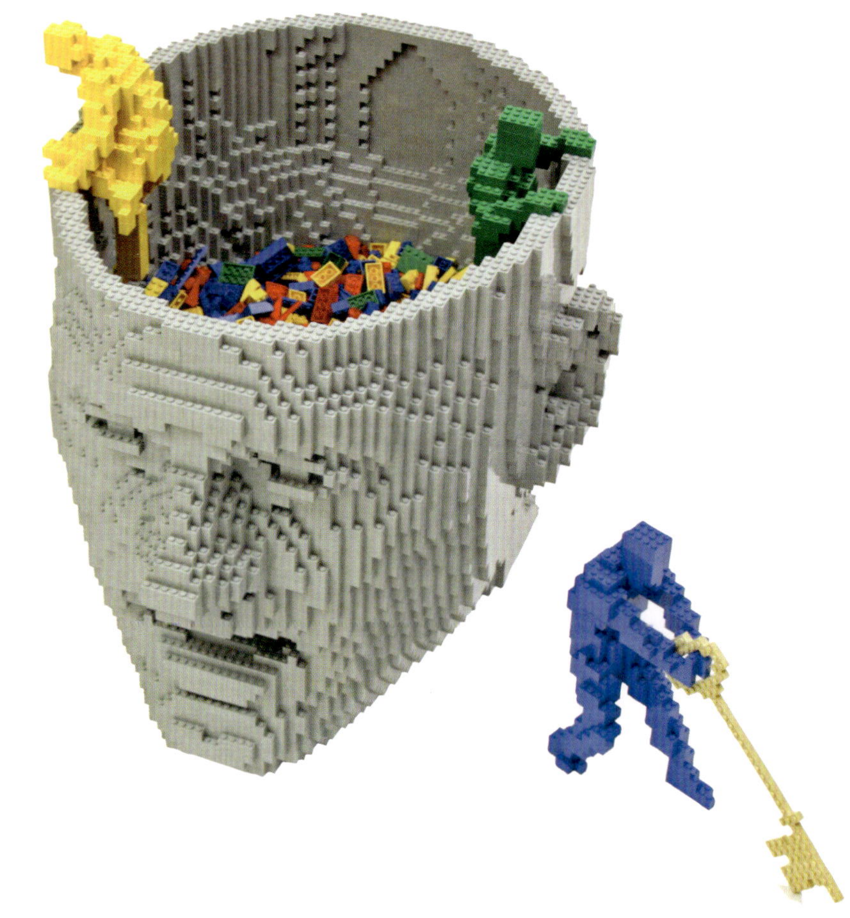

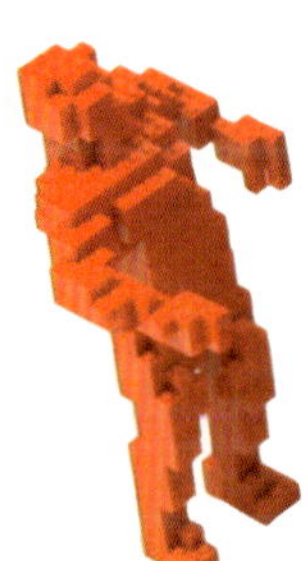

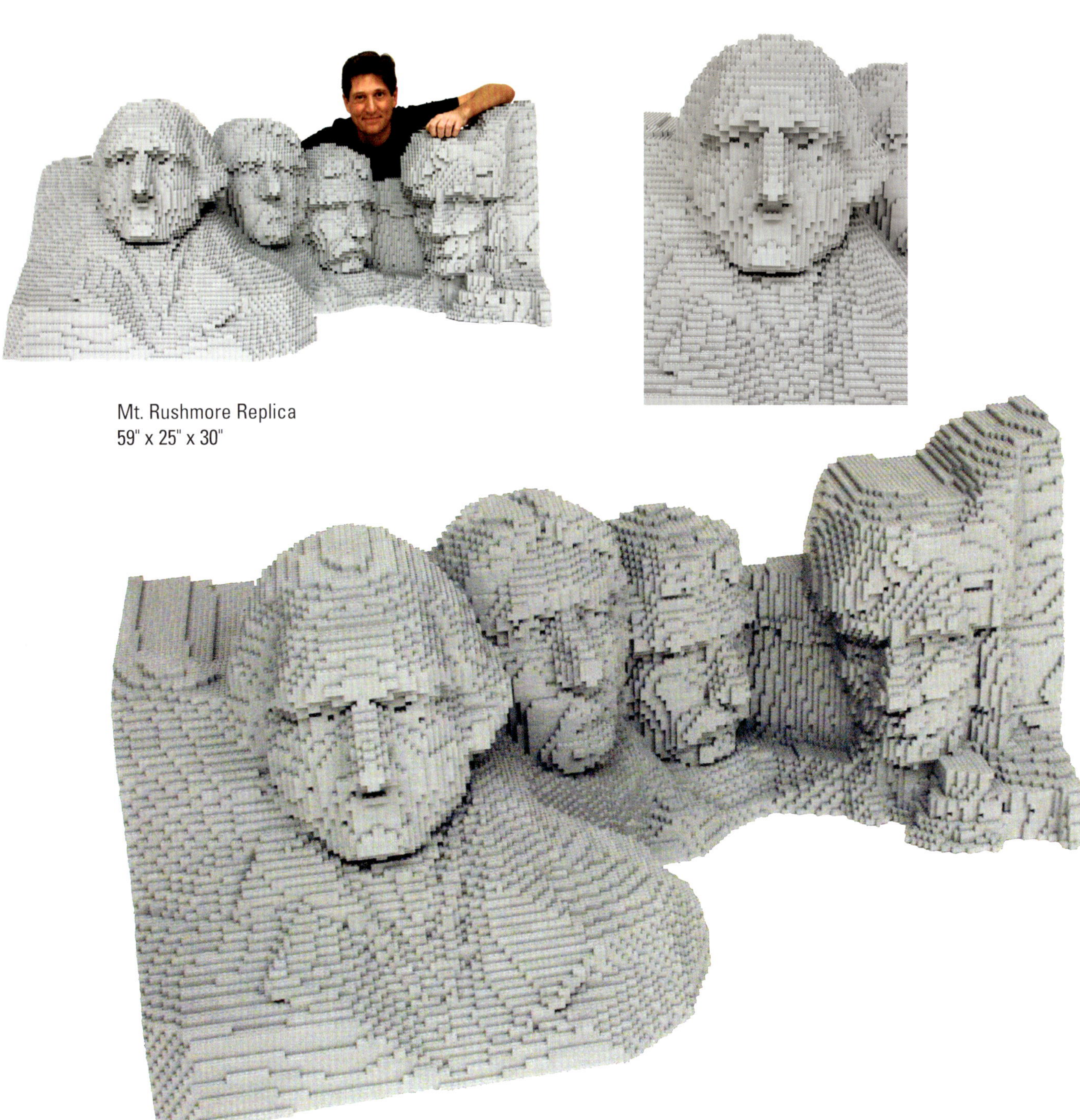

Mt. Rushmore Replica
59" x 25" x 30"

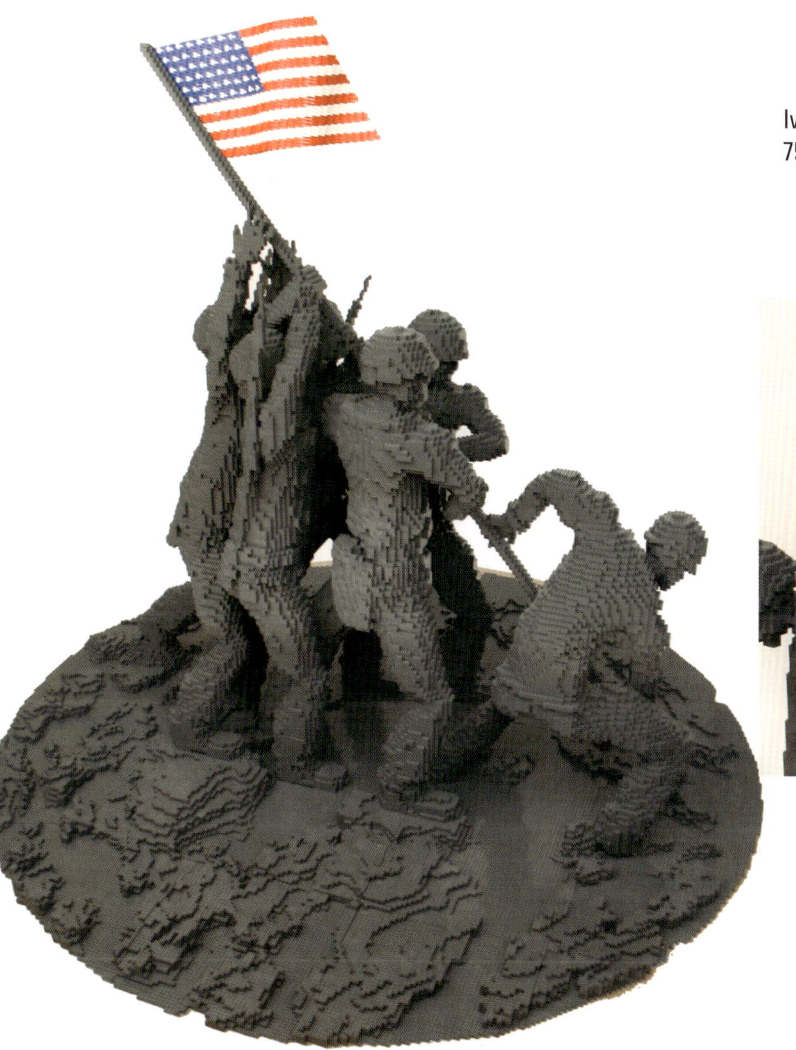

Iwo Jima Replica
75" x 75" x 68"

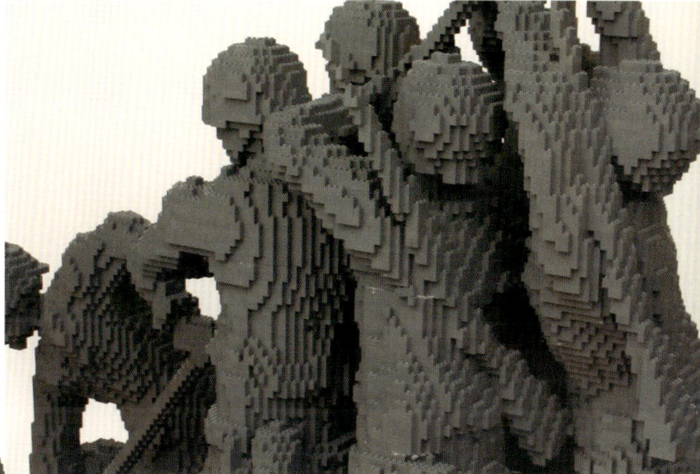

I was honored to be commissioned to build a replica of the flag raising at Iwo Jima for permanent installation at the National Museum of the Marine Corps. Using Joe Rosenthal's famous photograph as inspiration, I sculpted the five Marines and a Navy corpsman raising the flag atop Mount Suribachi during the Battle of Iwo Jima. The sculpture used over 100,000 bricks.

Eileen Fisher Outfit
50" x 18" x 13"

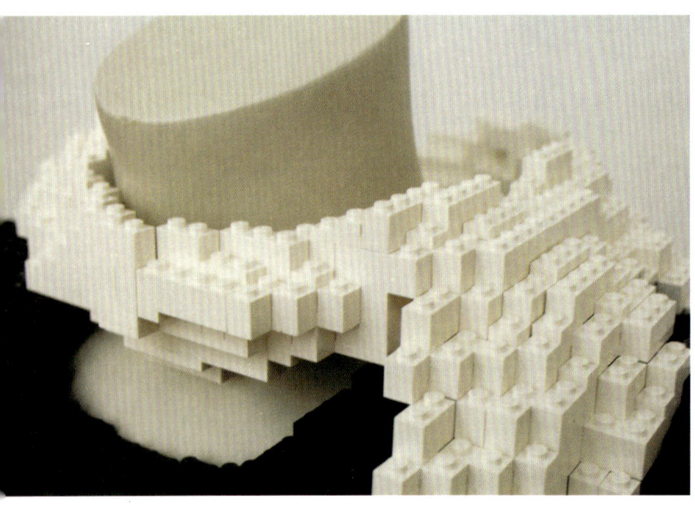

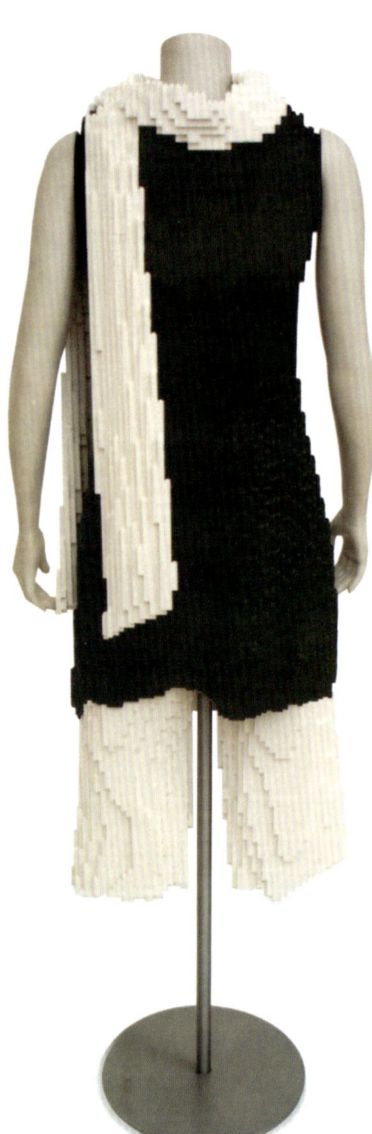

Just for the record, this brick outfit is a bit painful to wear and will cause chafing in certain places. I know.

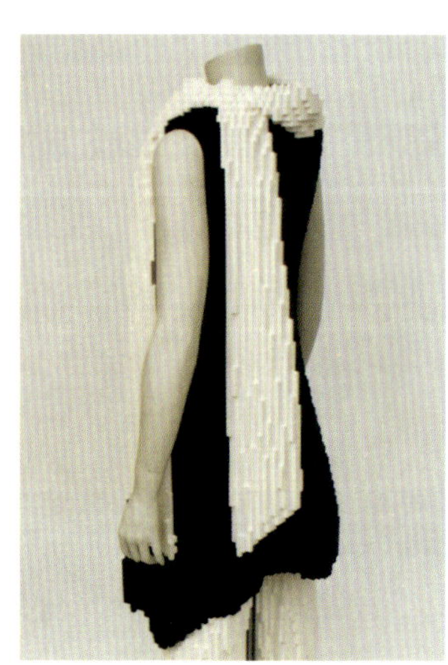

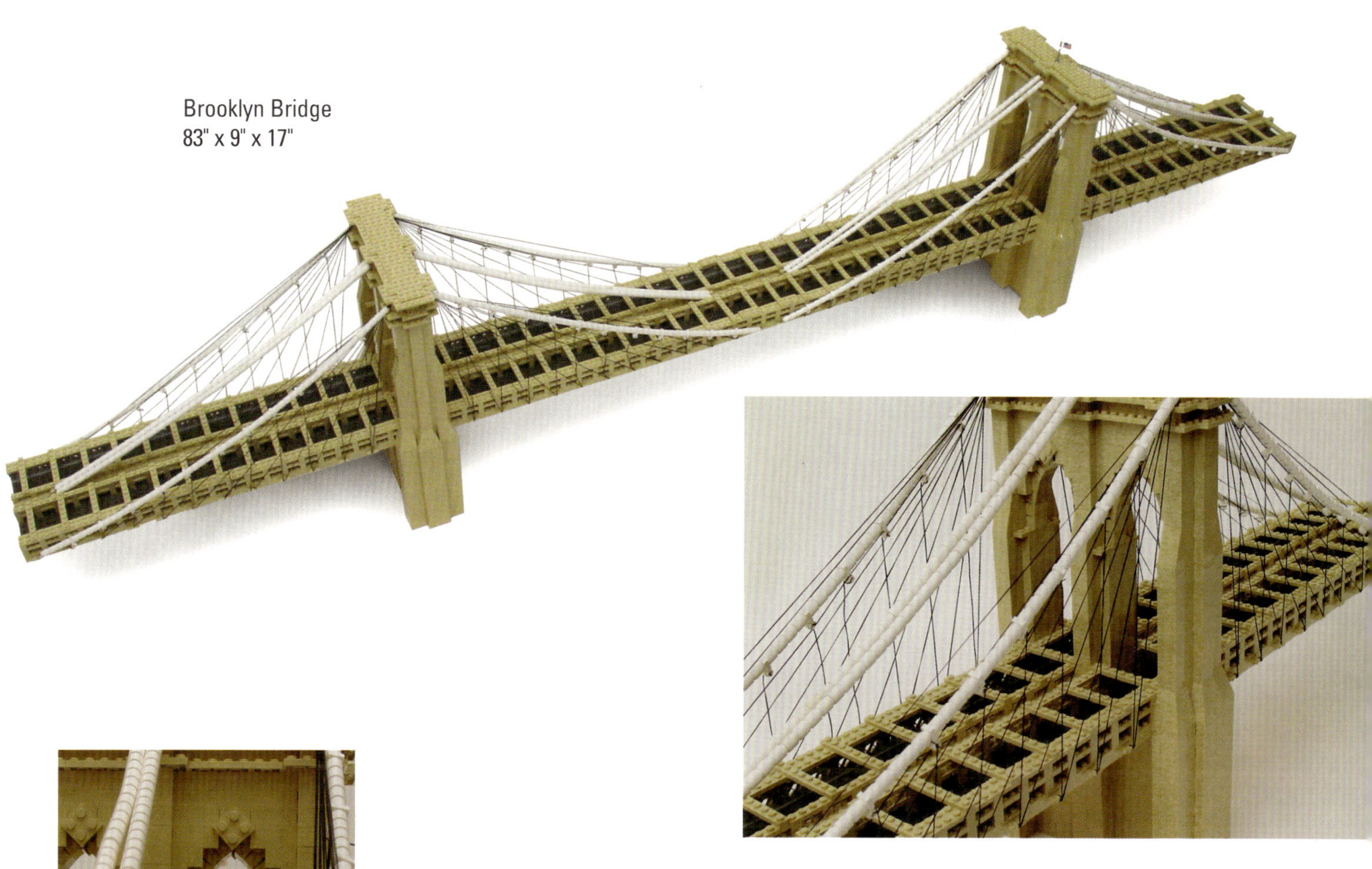

Brooklyn Bridge
83" x 9" x 17"

Young Basketball Player
32" x 52" x 22"

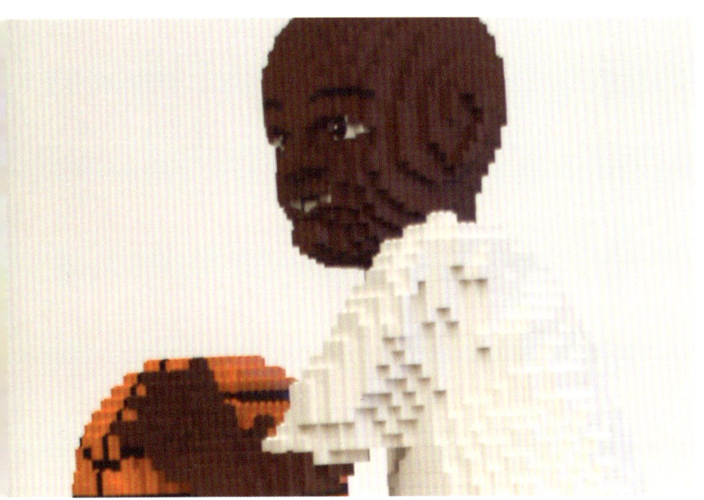

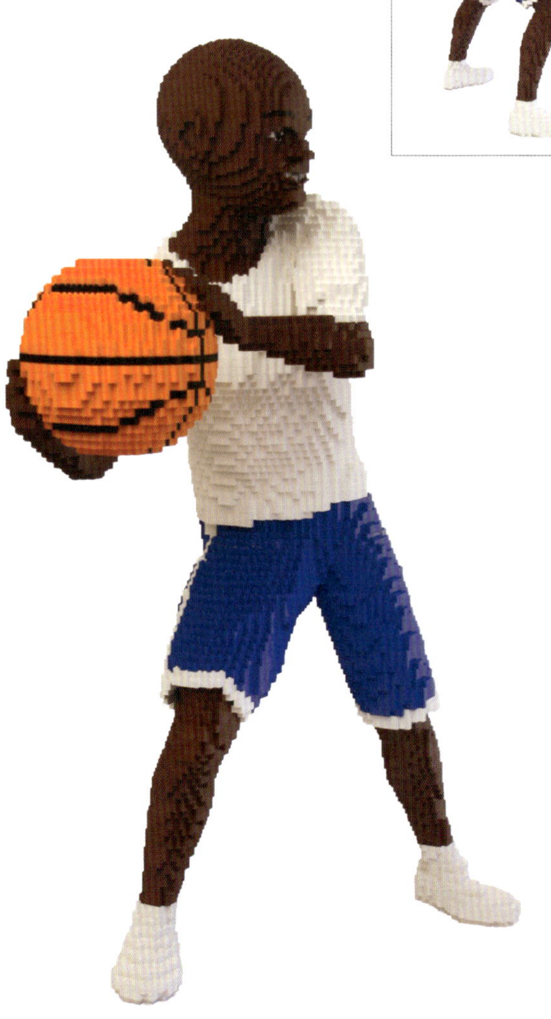

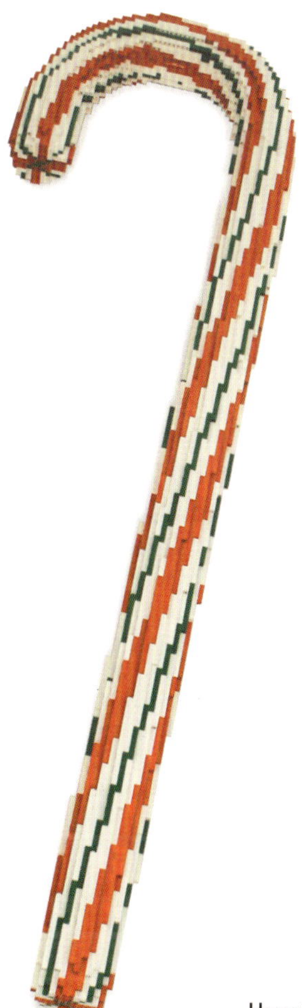

Candy Cane
68" x 20" x 5"

I was running out of green bricks during this project.
As I neared the top and end of the cane, I realized I was going to be about three bricks short. I decided to keep building and amazingly I had just enough bricks to finish. It was a Christmas miracle. Or I counted wrong.

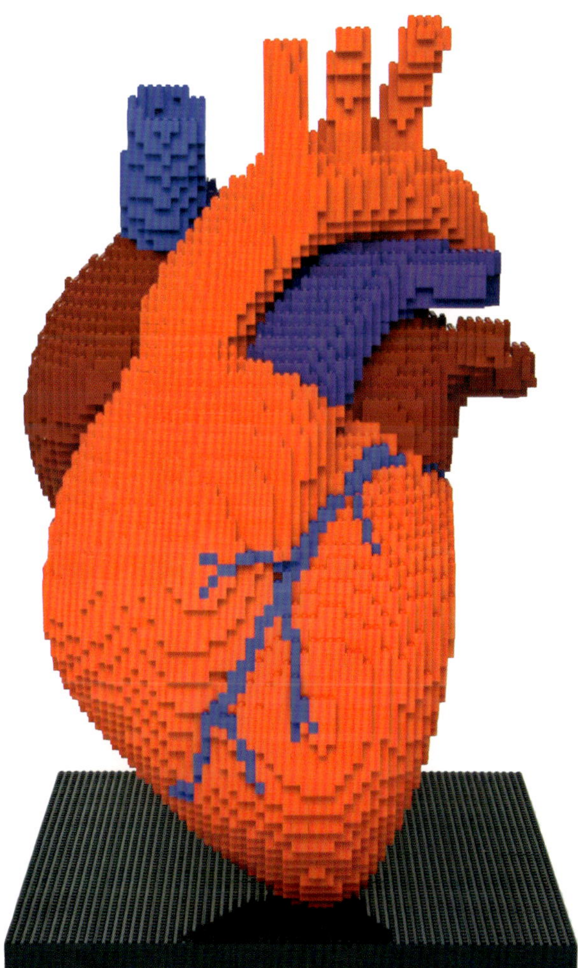

Heart
20" x 32" x 20"

Built for a children's hospital to help doctors explain how the heart works to their young patients.

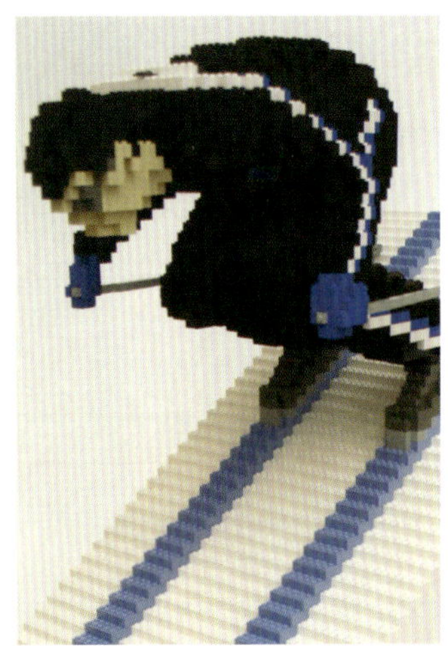

Skier
28" x 15" x 34"

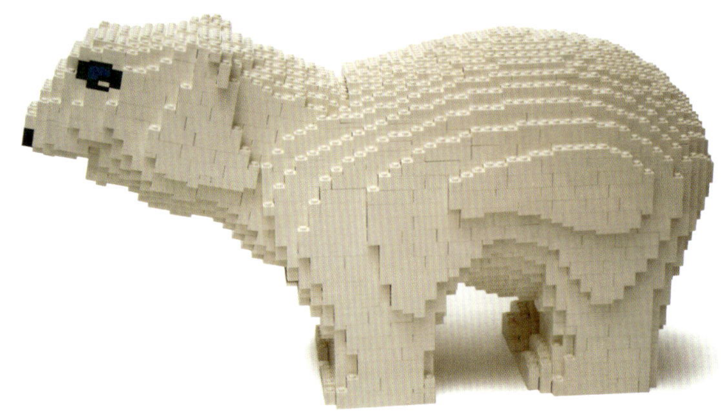

Polar bear
11" x 20" x 8"

This project made me very happy and euphoric while I was working. However, at certain points, it became very difficult and I become quite sad. Later, I returned to a manic state of elation as I neared the finish. But when it was done, I felt depressed that it was over. I call this project my bipolar bear.

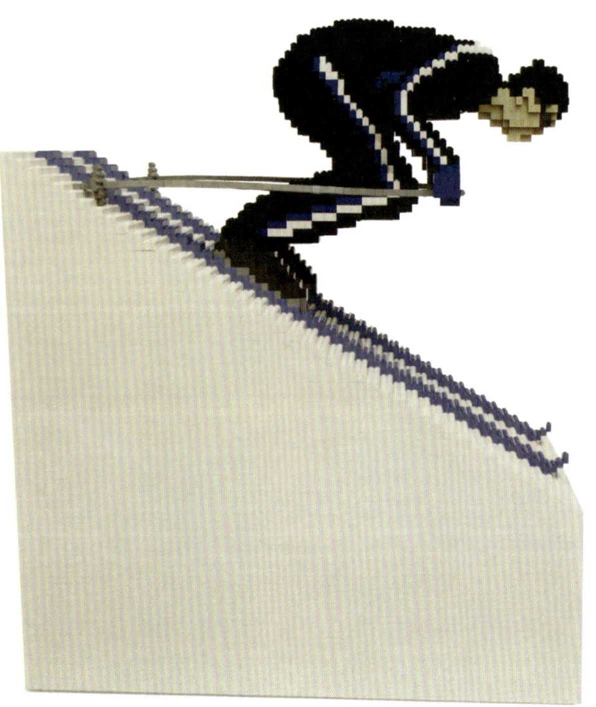

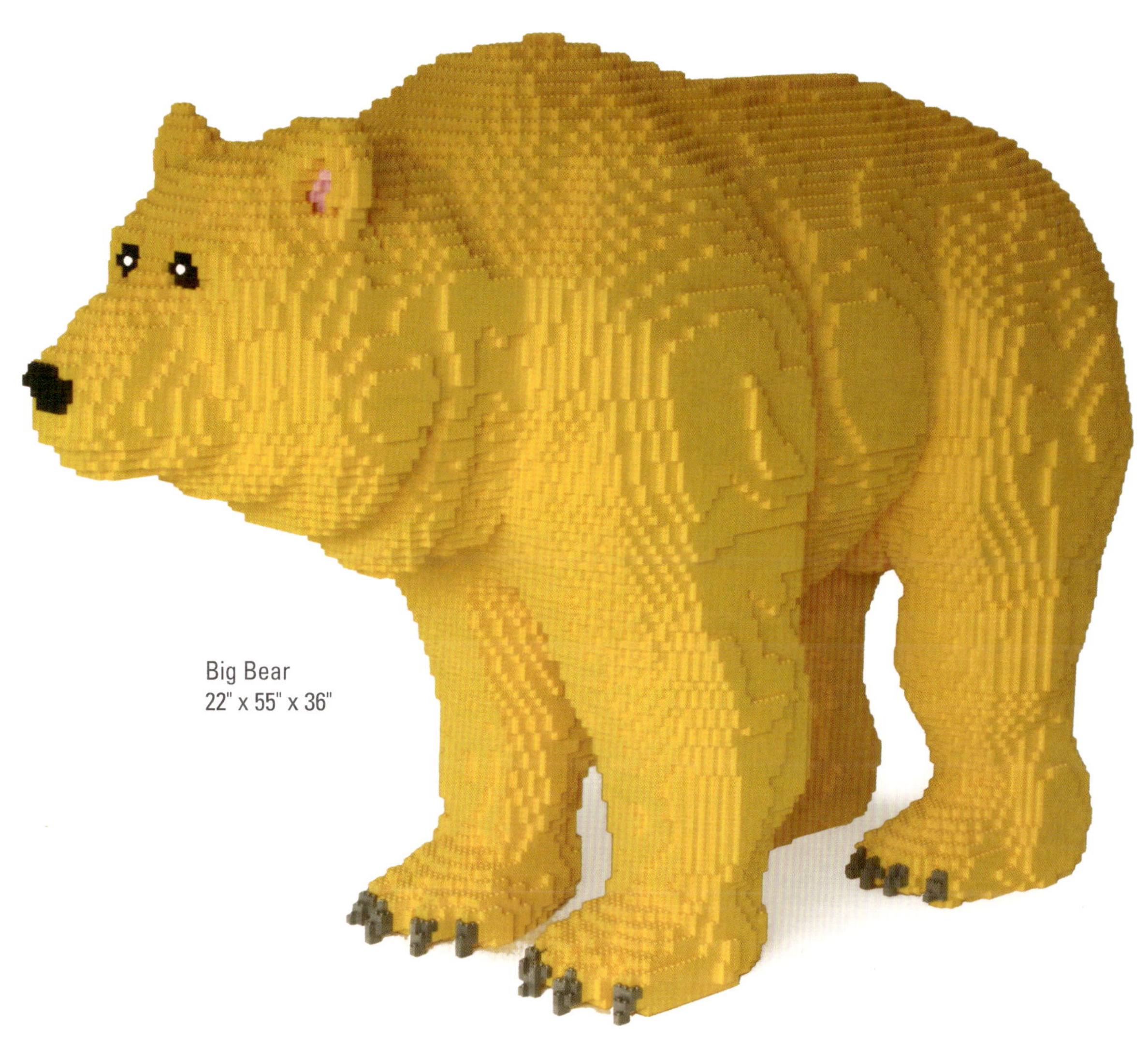

Big Bear
22" x 55" x 36"

Skull
29" x 18" x 14"

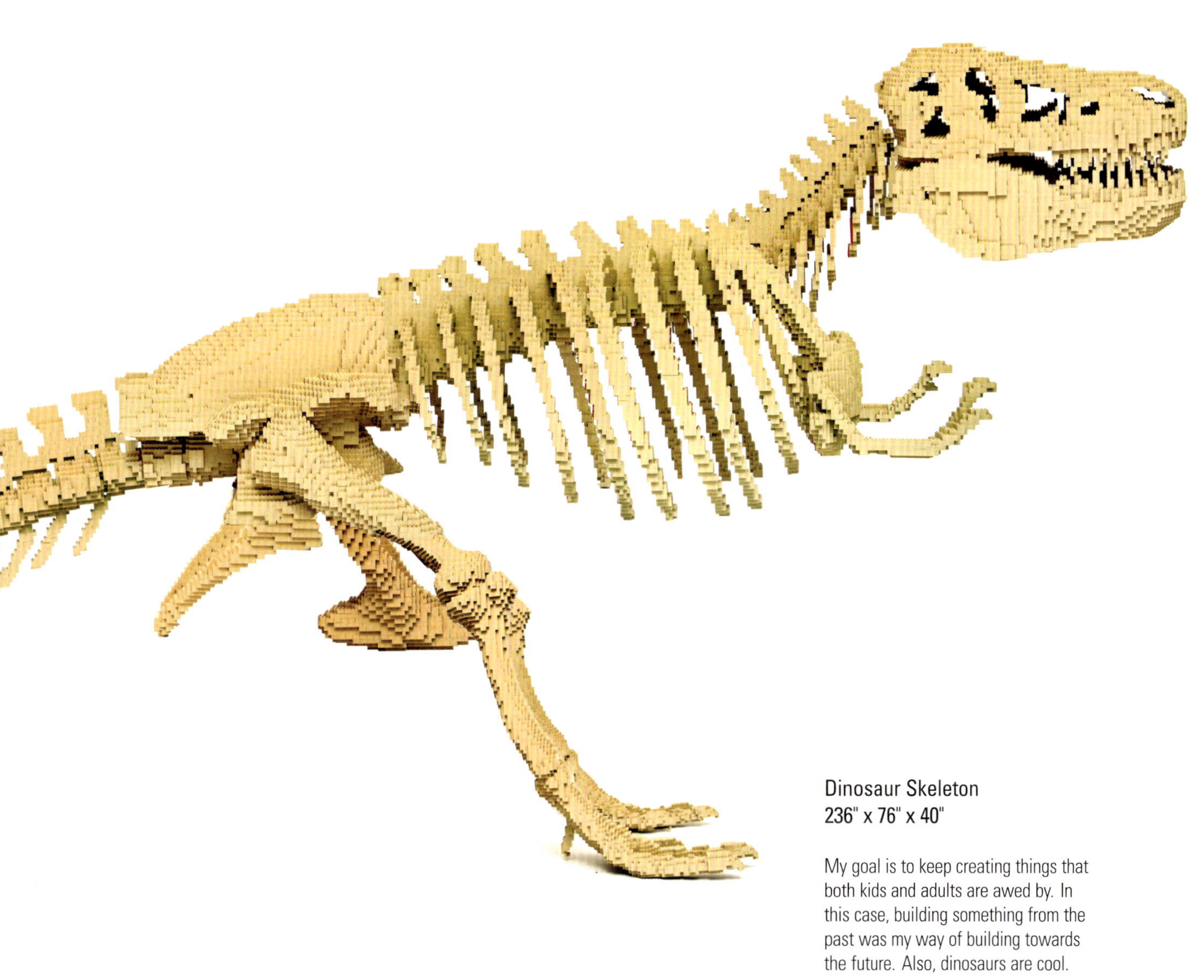

Dinosaur Skeleton
236" x 76" x 40"

My goal is to keep creating things that both kids and adults are awed by. In this case, building something from the past was my way of building towards the future. Also, dinosaurs are cool.

About Nathan Sawaya

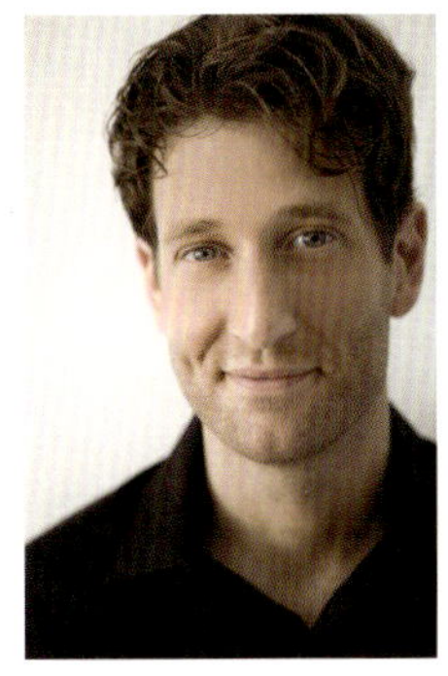

NATHAN SAWAYA BRICK ARTIST™

Nathan Sawaya is a New York-based artist who creates awe-inspiring works out of some of the most unlikely things. His art focuses on large-scale sculptures using only toy building blocks: LEGO bricks to be exact.

For years, Nathan's touring exhibit – The Art of the Brick – has entertained and inspired millions of art lovers and enthusiasts around the globe. It is the only exhibition focusing exclusively on LEGO as an art medium. The creations, constructed from nearly one million pieces, were built from standard bricks beginning as early as 2000.

Born in Colville, Washington and raised in Veneta, Oregon, Sawaya's childhood dreams were always fun and creative. He drew cartoons, wrote stories, perfected magic tricks and of course also played with LEGO. His days were filled with imagination. But when it came time for college, Sawaya moved to New York City and attended NYU. He attended NYU School of Law and became an attorney. But soon he realized he would rather be sitting on the floor expressing himself with LEGO bricks, than sitting in a board room negotiating contracts.

It was then that Sawaya rediscovered his beloved LEGO bricks and indulged in his inner child to create what many believe is a new art revolution using LEGO as an art medium.

Today Sawaya has more than 1.5 million colored bricks in his New York art studio. His work is obsessively and painstakingly crafted and is both beautiful and playful. Sawaya's ability to transform LEGO bricks into something new, his devotion to scale and color perfection, the way he conceptualizes the action of the subject matter, enables him to elevate an ordinary toy to the status of fine art.

Sawaya's art form takes shape primarily in 3-dimensional sculptures and oversized portraits. He continues to create daily with the brick medium while accepting commission work from individuals and corporations requesting works of art, looking for unique, eye-catching exhibits.

For more information about Nathan Sawaya and his artwork, visit www.brickartist.com.

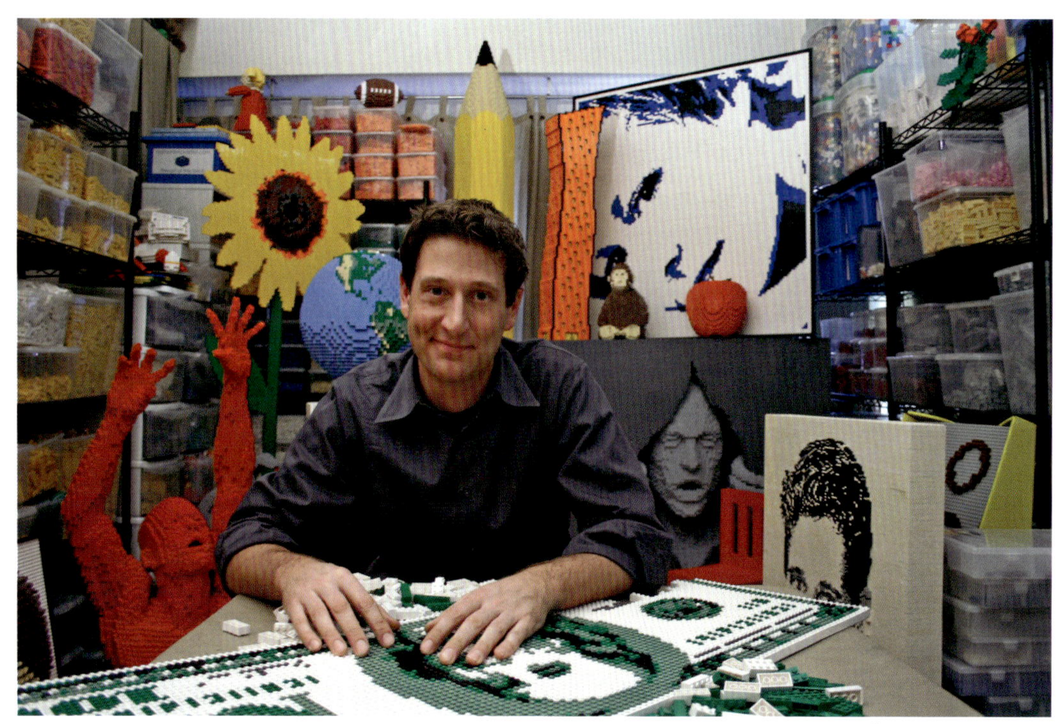

To see more of Nathan Sawaya's artwork, visit www.brickartist.com.